KUNDALINI WARNING

ARE FALSE SPIRITS INVADING THE CHURCH?

(2015 UPDATE)

ANDREW STROM

Revival School

1

KUNDALINI WARNING

Published by: RevivalSchool

www.revivalschool.com

Wholesale distribution by Lightning Source, Inc.

ISBN-13: 978-0-9799073-9-5

ISBN-10: 0-9799073-9-X

Prophets -- History 2. Revivals

A NOTE ON THE AUTHORS

Fergus Henderson trained as an architect before becoming a chef. He opened the French House Dining Room in 1992 and left it to start St. John in 1994. He is the author of the cult classic *Nose to Tail Eating*, which won the André Simon Award in 1999.

Justin Piers Gellatly is Head Baker and Pastry Chef at both St. John and St. John Bread & Wine. He began working with Fergus Henderson in 2000 behind the stoves at St. John, but after volunteering to do extra baking and pastry shifts, decided to move across permanently to the pastry kitchen. He has never looked back.

CONTENTS

CHAPTER ONE

HOW FAR THE FALL

To avoid misunderstanding, let me be clear before I begin. I am not writing this as an "outsider." I have been part of the Charismatic movement for more than 30 years – and I was involved with the modern "Prophetic" movement for over a decade. So I am not coming at this from the 'outside' pointing the finger. But there are things in our movement that have become utterly sick and ungodly. Who could deny it? In fact, I know of many people who no longer want to be labeled as "Charismatic" at all. Is it possible that the "invasion" of bizarre and unbiblical goings-on that we have seen in the last 20 years is behind a lot of this? That is what the following pages seek to uncover.

So where do we begin? Well, picture this. It is 2010. There are two leaders on stage at a large Christian event. But this is no ordinary gathering. The men appear to be reeling drunk or – literally – "stoned". Yet the Christians in the audience are shouting their approval – laughing uproariously. Amazingly, one of the men on stage is puffing on something that looks almost like a Marijuana joint – at least that is the impression he gives as he staggers around the stage. But it is not actually Marijuana. It is a little plastic "Jesus" doll that he is puffing on – and he calls this "Toking the Ghost." The men are urging the crowd to do the same – to become 'drunk in the spirit' by "toking the Ghost" like they are. And many are following suit.

Who are these men? They are John Crowder (the self-described "New Mystic") and his partner-in-crime Ben Dunn. Welcome to the new face of the 'River' movement. These are the men behind "Sloshfest" and the 'Drunken Glory' Tours. And their influence has grown enormously in the Charismatic movement – especially amongst the youth.

Anyone who thinks that this is just some small "fringe" group needs to think again. In recent years, one or other of these guys has shared the stage with such Charismatic stars as James Goll, Heidi Baker, Cal Pierce (of 'Healing Rooms' fame), Bobby Conner or Patricia King. Crowder is a friend and admirer of Todd Bentley. And his partner Ben Dunn has been invited to teach at Bill Johnson's famous Bethel School of Ministry in Redding, California. These guys are now real "names" in the movement. Crowder's book "The New Mystics" became a big hit among those who see themselves as part of the 'River' renewal.

John Crowder's own website advertised his Training School as follows:

"Savor the deep things of the Spirit ...

Our Mystical School is an intensive, three-day course with in-depth instruction, activation and hands-on impartation with John Crowder... In these courses you will:

Operate in Trances, Raptures & Ecstatic Prayer

Experience Physical Phenomena of Mysticism

Get Activated in Creative Miracles, Signs & Wonders

Understand & Access New Creation Realities

Gain A Historical Grid of Miracle Workers & Mystics

Be Activated in the Seer Realm, Prophecy, Spirit Travel

Receive Open Heavens & Revelatory Understanding

Access and Manifest the Glory Realm... "

I don't know about you, but I doubt that even a Hindu Guru could manage to sound more "New Age" than the above list! And yet John Crowder is a rising star in today's Charismatic movement!

Even the editor of Charisma magazine, Lee Grady, began asking some pointed questions: *"The spiritual drunkenness craze led to other charismatic fads, including an infatuation with angels, an obsession with golden dust and the strange teachings of John Crowder—a confessed "new mystic" who compares the infilling of the Holy Spirit to smoking marijuana.*

Crowder, who is planting a church in Santa Cruz, Calif., this fall, sometimes calls his meetings "sloshfests" and refers to himself as a bartender for God. He teaches that God wants all Christians to be continually drunk in the Holy Spirit—and he provides resources to help you do just that, including an electronica recording that will help you, in Crowder's words, "trance out," and a teaching that encourages stigmata and levitation.

I'll let the theologians sort out all the obvious reasons why Crowder and other "new mystics" are treading on dangerous ground. Meanwhile I have a less complicated concern. With all of this emphasis on Holy Ghost intoxication, did anybody notice that the Bible clearly commands us to be spiritually sober?"

But clearly these guys are not remotely concerned about biblical injunctions toward sobriety. They just laugh off any criticism as coming from religious "Pharisees" – and carry on regardless. At least, that is the general response that I have seen over the years. And it seems to be getting worse.

In January 2010 David Lowe, a journalist for the Sun newspaper in England, was asked along to the UK Sloshfest. Below are some of his observations:

"Sloshfest organiser David Vaughan... makes no apologies for painting God as a party animal who wants to win over youngsters with supernatural highs... "Heaven is going to be wild. God will show up and be the life of the party... "

Christians who claim to get high on the Holy Spirit and drunk on Heaven's wine have caused outrage in the USA. Dozens of complaints about blasphemy have been posted on YouTube videos of the movement's best-known advocate, John Crowder. The former alcoholic, whose fans are dubbed "Crowderites", is at

Sloshfest and typically slurs through sermons about "smoking the Baby Jesus", being "whacked out" and "tokin' on the Holy Ghost".

Amid the chaos a woman dressed as a pirate queen crawls past muttering. Strangely, despite no sign of alcohol or drugs being consumed, she and many other worshippers look spaced out, with red, puffy eyes and a vacant stare..."

Speaking of the subject of "blasphemy", it is interesting to note what the well-known Charismatic teacher Derek Prince said:

"We are warned by Jesus Himself to be very, very careful how we speak about the Holy Spirit, how we represent the Holy Spirit. Jesus uses the word blasphemy, and I decided to look it up in my big Greek lexicon. The primary meaning of to blaspheme is given in the lexicon as this: to speak lightly or amiss of sacred things. So when you speak lightly or amiss concerning the Holy Spirit, or misrepresent the character of the Holy Spirit, by definition you are close to blaspheming.

If you have ever done that, or been prone to do it, or been associated with those who do it, I want to offer you some sincere advice: You need to repent. You need to settle that matter once and for all with God and never again be guilty of misrepresenting God's Holy Spirit. **For the Holy Spirit is holy and He is God.** *"*

Frankly, I agree with Derek Prince. A lot of the videos and material that John Crowder's "New Mystics" have posted on the Internet are literally so sick, demeaning and blasphemous to God and His Spirit, that I can hardly bring myself to watch them. So why has he rapidly become something of a "star" in the Charismatic scene? How did things ever come to this? How could something so sick and unholy come to appeal to so many in our movement?

We need to know exactly what happened to bring about such apostasy. Because Sloshfest and the New Mystics are not an isolated case. They are part of a vast array of similar ministries that have virtually taken over entire sections of the Prophetic and Charismatic movements. How could such a thing happen? What are the steps that led up to it? That is exactly what we are about to find out in this book.

BUT FIRST...

Before we look at what led us into this quagmire, it is important that I briefly talk about my own background – so you know where I am coming from. As noted earlier, I am a Spirit-filled, tongues-speaking Christian with a long involvement in both the Charismatic and Prophetic movements. In fact, I was involved in the same Prophetic movement as Todd Bentley, Rick Joyner, Paul Cain and Mike Bickle for over 11 years – though nowhere near their level of notoriety. (The Prophetic movement is a branch of the Charismatic movement that believes in modern "prophets and apostles"). But by 2004 things were getting so bad that I found I could no longer remain. In fact, I had to announce that I was leaving. I had come to see that I could only be part of a completely different kind of 'Prophetic' altogether – one that was calling the church back to repentance and holiness – to the purity and power of the early church. And this modern 'Prophetic' simply was not doing that.

My announcement in 2004 that I was leaving the Prophetic movement created an enormous firestorm – far greater than my participation ever had. I received literally thousands of emails from around the world – most of them agreeing with the stand I had taken. But many of the responses still shocked and saddened me. As I wrote in an article several weeks later:

It has not been the emails that disagree with me or accuse me of being "divisive", etc, that bring me to tears. It is the emails from all over the world that strongly AGREE with me and tell me of other horrors that they have witnessed themselves. I sat at my computer last night getting sadder and sadder as I read account after account of the sickness that has spread around the globe as part of this movement. -It is actually WORSE than I ever imagined...

We are talking here about a movement where it is encouraged for people to interact with "Orbs of light" that come hovering down (a major prophetic ministry does this) or to pay money for personal "dream interpretations". We are talking about a movement that teaches people how to "visualize" their way into the 'Third Heaven' and sometimes holds 'Presbytery' days where you can book a half-hour personal appointment with a prophet for a hefty fee. We are talking about a movement that majors on 'manifestations', "portals" and weird 'visitations'. In every way it more closely resembles the New Age movement than anything Christian. In fact, more and more I am seeing that this movement is utterly dominated by a spirit of DIVINATION and fortune-telling. It is sick beyond words. And its prophets are utterly blind. Even now, they rush to hold a huge 'Visitations' gathering in Hollywood...

I am close to tears even now, just writing about it. It is so awful what this movement has become. Please STAY AWAY from it, my friends. We are talking about DEMONIC encounters here. "And no marvel; for Satan himself is transformed into an angel of light. Therefore it is no great thing if his ministers also be transformed as the ministers of righteousness" (2 Cor 11:14-15). We truly are in the Last Days.

HOW THIS INVASION BEGAN

A lot of people don't realize the strong links between the "Toronto Blessing" and modern leaders like Todd Bentley or John Crowder. They are not aware of the massive ties between "Toronto", the modern 'Prophetic' movement, and things like the Lakeland revival or "Sloshfest." You need to know that every one of these movements and leaders is utterly interconnected. How do I know? Because I was part of the Prophetic movement for over 11 years. I had my ear to that Grapevine, so to speak, and I had to deal with each of these movements and leaders as they came along. I was totally aware of the interconnections. In fact, most people in that circle were very aware. The links are still very strong to this day, as we shall see.

10

But really, we need to go back one more step to truly understand where this "River" originated from – the common source. We need to go back to a rather rotund Prosperity preacher from South Africa who called himself the "Holy Ghost Bartender" – and who told his audiences to "Belly up to the bar and drink." We need to go back to a man named Rodney Howard-Browne.

The first time I remember seeing Howard-Browne was on a video in my home city of Auckland, New Zealand. The year was either 1993 or 1994, and at that time I was the editor of a small national Prophetic Bulletin in NZ. But what I saw on that video truly sickened me. They were touting it as a "revival" which Howard-Browne was leading in Florida, but I was so disturbed by what I saw that I told the lady that she ought not to be importing such "dangerous" material into the Body of Christ in New Zealand. And I started to realize that if there was going to be an "invasion" of such stuff, then I was going to have to speak out against it – a thought that literally filled me with dread. Little did I realize where all of this was going to lead.

For some months I managed to stay out of any real conflict, but then the "Toronto Blessing" became big news in the Christian media, and I simply had to speak out. I discovered that Toronto was simply the "Rodney Howard-Browne anointing" dressed up in different clothes. (In other words, Vineyard pastor Randy Clark had taken Howard-Browne's "anointing" into the Toronto Airport Vineyard church in early 1994 – and that's how the whole 'Blessing' movement started. The history of this is beyond dispute – and most people freely acknowledge Howard-Browne's role as the originator of "Toronto").

I had seen and investigated enough by this time to confirm my worst suspicions of what was going on. But still, my first attempts at exposing this "invasion" were fairly mild. Below are some extracts from my first article on this topic in New Zealand's national Christian newspaper, 'Challenge Weekly', dated August 26, 1994. I guess this was my first forlorn shot (of many) across the bows:

In recent weeks there has been some talk in the Christian media of what is known as the "laughing revival", which seems to be sweeping through the United States and parts of Canada. It has been present in NZ for some time also and I have been following its progress. It often seems to involve the preacher "blowing" on people, who then fall down laughing and shaking. I have seen video footage of one of the leading proponents of this movement, Rodney Howard Brown [sic], ministering in America. I have also been present to see another of these American 'laughing movement' leaders minister in Auckland recently.

I have to admit that there are many aspects of what I have seen that have greatly disturbed me. One of the things that has alarmed me most, is the fact that some of the leaders of this movement seem to be referring to it as a "revival" or a 'new move of God', but this `laughing' movement does not line up at all with the many specific things that God has been showing people in New Zealand about the coming Revival. Or in any real way with the great moves of God in the past.

For some years now, I have studied many accounts of past revivals where certain features have repeated themselves time and time again... History shows that revival begins with the Christians being brought to their knees. It is a flood of deep conviction, purging and repentance aimed at "cleaning out" the church and restoring her to New Testament purity and power.

As well as speaking of the flood of deep repentance that is coming, God has also been showing many praying people that a great "shaking" is about to come upon the church.

Regarding the current "laughing" movement, I have been greatly disturbed by what I have seen of it. Counterfeits abound in times of Revival. My greatest fear is that this `laughing' movement will spread right through the churches with few real questions being asked, simply because it has been accepted elsewhere.

I would urge all Christians to exercise great discernment regarding this movement and others like it. I believe a genuine Revival is coming, and it is dangerous to settle for anything less...

Needless to say, my article had about as much effect on the "invasion" as a gnat biting the rear of an elephant. But at least there were a few (small) voices being raised against it. Little did I know how bad things were going to get – or how lonely I was going to be made to feel.

'TORONTO' FLOODS IN

Now the "invasion" began in earnest. I truly believe that this movement infected the Commonwealth nations far more than it did the USA. In other words, it had a far wider effect on the Charismatic/ Pentecostal churches in the UK, Australia and New Zealand, etc, that it did in the United States. This is because there are far more Conservative Evangelicals in the USA, plus entire separate denominations such as Pentecostal Holiness, etc, which hardly even felt it at all. But in my home country of New Zealand, it left virtually nobody unscathed.

Down came the big "Blessing" leaders from North America. Both Rodney Howard-Browne and John Arnott (the main Toronto leader) held huge meetings in New Zealand. So did lesser-knowns such as Jill Austin from Kansas City – whom I actually came to regard as more dangerous and extreme still. I once attended a Jill Austin meeting where people were being bodily thrown as much as 10 feet (some had even landed on children) and the room was full of people making giant "bat-like" movements and an eerie wailing noise. It was not far off a horror movie! And you literally left these meetings feeling utterly grieved and sick in your spirit. What an awful time.

Virtually every Charismatic or Pentecostal pastor in New Zealand was into this movement. Even many from the Assemblies of God – and other so-called "conservative" Pentecostals! And even some of the Baptists! It was a nightmare.

13

Entire meetings would be spent, week after week, in seeking strange "experiences". Whole churches would be convulsed with hyena-like laughter, "drunken" antics, jerking, barking, roaring, and animal-like convulsions. It was like a lunatic asylum - it really was. Everybody was "soaking" in this new anointing. Everybody was doing 'carpet time'. It got to the point where you didn't dare let anyone lay on hands and pray for you any more. The invasion was complete. It occurred on literally an epidemic scale. And soon there were hardly any leaders left – even "little" guys – who would dare speak up against it. This was especially true in Charismatic and Pentecostal circles. A friend and I used to joke darkly that it was like the old movie, "Invasion of the Body Snatchers." They seemed to have "snatched" almost all of our friends, and now they were coming for us.

THE BIG LEADERS

I am convinced that one of the biggest factors in the spread of 'Toronto' around the world was "peer pressure" – especially at a leadership level. The very biggest Charismatic leaders all seemed to be into it, so why not jump on board? And a great deal of pressure was put on anybody who dared to disagree.

There only seemed to be a miniscule number of Charismatic leaders around the world who spoke up against it – and most of these were "half-unknown" guys. Art Katz wrote one article cautioning about Toronto (but not Brownsville) and we heard that Derek Prince had made a tape where he spoke against "animal manifestations," etc. Another leader named Clifford Hill from the UK gave some very strong warnings. But by and large, it was a complete walkover. We only learned after his death how strongly Derek Prince had spoken out – because only then were his comments seemingly published in accessible form – in a book entitled "Protection From Deception." But we never had access to this in the crucial years when it really mattered. Most of us felt like we had to face the invasion virtually alone. But I did publish what information came to hand.

Of course, there were always the anti-Charismatic leaders such as Hank Hanegraaff and John MacArthur who could be relied upon to speak against the whole thing. But very few from the Spirit-filled camp listened to these guys – because they were already known to be virulently anti-Charismatic and therefore "biased."

Ironically, one of the first big leaders to speak out strongly against this invasion was Benny Hinn! The Word-of-Faith camp had earlier embraced Rodney Howard Browne and his strange "manifestations." (After all, he was a huge 'Prosperity' preacher). There had even been a famous video of Kenneth Copeland welcoming Rodney and his "drunken laughter" on television – with all kinds of silly antics between the two of them.

But in July 1997, Benny Hinn spoke out strongly on the PTL television show. Several of his comments are below:

"Some of what is happening today, some of these manifestations where people are barking, making sounds of animals - I can tell you, that is not the Holy Spirit. It is purely demonic. The Holy Ghost does not bark. Only a devil barks. If somebody barks in my meeting, I'll cast the devil out of that man...

Much of what happens is pure emotionalism - contagious laughter. What does it do except make you look stupid? I am not interested in some emotional up. All I want is the power of Almighty God that will transform your life...

I've never known Jesus to bark. Have you? Can you imagine Peter the apostle barking in the book of Acts? But you know why some have accepted such nonsense? Because they're not grounded. They are not grounded. Don't you dare experiment with anything. If it's not in the Bible, don't do it!...

I asked Dr. Summerall before he died. I said, "Dr. Summerall, what do you think of all these things happening, people barking and doing all these things?"

"Devils, devils," he said. "Devils."

Did Benny Hinn's comments have any effect at all on the spread of this movement? Not that I could tell. And anyway, by 1997 the damage was almost all done. The movement had spread just about as far as it could spread.

Another thing that had taken place earlier should have set off even louder alarm bells with leaders worldwide. In December 1995, the Toronto Airport Vineyard church (home of the 'Toronto Blessing') had been expelled from the international Vineyard movement. This expulsion came after what had apparently been twelve months of repeated warnings given to the Toronto church by John Wimber and the Vineyard Association. But did any of this do enough to stop the "invasion"? Sadly not. There were many years of havoc to play out yet.

PROFOUND CHANGES

Meanwhile, in 1996 I turned 30 years old, and there came a change in my ministry that I had no idea would literally transform my future and send me around the world. What happened in 1996 was that we launched our first 'Revival' website on the Internet – which was only in its infancy at that time. Our first website was colored gray (exciting!) and had a very basic design. But right from the start people were drawn to the outspoken call that we issued – to repentance and holiness – to true Prophetic preaching and real Revival. Very soon people were getting in touch from all over the world.

We also started our international Email List that same year, and before we knew it 300 people had joined. Soon it was up to 1000. Today it is called the 'REVIVAL' List and has over 17,000 members worldwide.

A man named Steve Schultz joined our List in those early days – but he didn't seem to much appreciate our call to Repentance or our attitude towards Toronto. He ended up leaving to start his own List – today called the "Elijah List" - which was to focus on publishing prophecies by the 'big names' and selling their books,

CD's, DVD's, etc. For a time the Elijah List greatly outgrew our own List, but lately it seems to have fallen on hard times somewhat. Is there something going on with the Prophetic movement that is causing this? Only time will tell.

TO CORRECT PUBLICLY OR PRIVATELY?

For years when I was discussing these issues I often avoided "naming names" as much as I could. Of course, some Christians claim that any correction or questioning of ministries should always be done PRIVATELY anyway - and only to the leaders concerned - never in public. (It is important to note that many such approaches have indeed been made to these leaders over the years. They have basically been ignored). But either way, I am afraid I cannot agree that public deception is only to be opposed behind closed doors.

We must not forget that in the New Testament the elders were commanded to correct severely (Titus 1:13) and to rebuke for sin publicly (1 Tim 5:20), though in 2 Tim 2:24-26 they were instructed to correct with 'meekness'. Remember, the apostle Paul rebuked Peter publicly in Galatians 2 for his hypocrisy, Jesus rebuked Peter openly in Matthew, and He even whipped the sellers out of the temple publicly in Mark (for making God's house a 'den of thieves'). In extreme cases the apostle Paul actually wrote to everyone that he was turning people over to Satan for correction (see 1 Cor 5 and 1 Tim 1:20). The Bible is very clear that one of our major tasks is to "expose" the deeds of darkness (Eph 5:11). In 1 Cor 4:21 Paul asks the people, "Shall I come to you with a rod, or in love?" The same apostle used 'boldness' in 2 Cor 10:1 and said that he would not spare anyone in 2 Cor 13:1-2.

Many Christians insist on applying Matt 18:15-17 to every situation. But what about false teachers? The above passage in Matt 18 says that if my brother "sins against me" then I should go to him privately about it - then with one or two witnesses - and then to the whole church if he does not repent. This is a very important process for resolving issues where a brother has sinned against me personally. But what about FALSE TEACHING of a serious nature? What if it is spreading or starting to infect entire sections of the body of Christ? Is it still just a "private matter"?

My understanding is that in the New Testament we NEVER see Jesus or the apostles treating false teaching as a "Matt 18" scenario. We see them publicly rebuking and correcting - trying to arrest the 'cancer' before it spreads any further. This is an act of LOVE towards the body. It is trying to stop the damage before too many precious sheep are harmed. False teaching and false prophets are never treated "nicely" or "sweetly" in the New Testament! (By the way, I am not advocating today's "heresy hunters", whom I believe often go about things with entirely the wrong spirit. But I am just laying down a few biblical guidelines here).

This is certainly an important issue in these Last Days, when we are told that false prophets and false teachers will 'abound', and that the deception will become so great that "if possible it would deceive the very elect." It is vital that we get a grasp of what is at stake here. The false teachers and false prophets in Acts were rebuked very bluntly, and Paul even "named names" in some of his letters to the churches. So surely we cannot continue to claim that this is all a "Matt 18" situation? Surely it is more serious than that - and requires a more drastic response? Of course, we must always be "speaking the truth in love" – and have the protection of Christ's precious sheep uppermost. But surely we must speak out and even "name names" if we see real danger to the Body? I trust and pray that we will do so in the right spirit in this book.

CHAPTER TWO
KUNDALINI – WHAT IS IT??

As we saw in the first chapter, there is a real Eastern/'New Age' sense to a lot of the stuff that has invaded the church in recent years. And of course, the term 'Kundalini' comes directly out of Eastern mysticism. This is a term that we certainly need to explore.

Back when we launched our Internet site in 1996, one of the first things we put on there was my article entitled, "The Toronto Controversy – Disturbing New Facts from History." Below is the opening paragraph to that article. I'm sure you will see why it caused such a reaction!:

"In this article, a Revival historian, closely aligned with the Charismatic and prophetic movements, raises the following questions: Why do the Toronto manifestations seem literally identical to many counterfeit movements which have destroyed genuine Revivals down through history? And why are they seemingly identical to the Chinese occultic 'Qigong' movement, as well as Franz Mesmer's occultic healing practice and the manifestations found throughout the "Kundalini" cults of Rajneesh, Ramakrishna, etc? Why are such manifestations found throughout the New Age movement worldwide, and yet nowhere in the Bible? If these are the days of "great deception" amongst Christians spoken of in the Bible, then shouldn't we be a little more careful about what we allow into God's church?"

As you can see, the connections between the Toronto/ "River" movement and this Hindu 'Kundalini' spirit were already being discussed way back in 1996. In fact, many observers who were aware of these Hindu/ New Age manifestations were immediately struck with the obvious similarity. Where exactly had Rodney Howard-Browne obtained his "anointing"? Of course, he claimed he received it in Africa and that it was from God. But why then was it so different from the Bible and yet so similar to the New Age – and the spirits that Hindu gurus operated under? This 'Kundalini' connection seemed a very obvious one to make. As I wrote in that same article:

A number of Indian gurus, such as Bagwhan Shree Rajneesh and Ramakrishna, have had the power to transfer a state of rapturous bliss to their followers merely by touching them. In the case of Ramakrishna, these states were often accompanied by uncontrollable laughter or weeping. Swami Baba Muktananda also had this power, according to a former devotee, and the resulting `Kundalini' manifestations included uncontrollable laughing, roaring, barking, crying, shaking, etc. Some of his followers also became mute or unconscious, while many felt themselves infused with feelings of tremendous joy, peace and love.

All such experiences have been based on "yielding" oneself to the power working through these gurus. Is it any coincidence that the manifestations associated with these demonic `Kundalini' cults are almost identical to those of Toronto?

KUNDALINI AWAKENINGS

If you search for Kundalini or Shakti on the Internet, you will find that multitudes of people in the New Age and Eastern religions still experience these powerful manifestations. As we know, this is often with the help of a Guru, who touches them on the forehead (this is called 'Shaktipat') – so that these people can experience a "Kundalini Awakening".

As researcher Robert Walker wrote in 1995:

"Few Christians realise that for thousands of years gurus have operated with gifts of healing, miracles, gifts of knowledge, and intense displays of spiritual consciousness as they stretch out and connect with a cosmic power which, though demonic in origin, is very real. The meetings which mystic Hindu gurus hold are called 'Darshan'. At these meetings devotees go forward to receive

spiritual experience from a touch by the open palm of the hand, often to the forehead, by the guru in what is known as the Shakti Pat or divine touch. The raising of the spiritual experience is called raising Kundalini... After a period when the devotee has reached a certain spiritual elevation they begin to shake, jerk, or hop or squirm uncontrollably, sometimes breaking into uncontrolled animal noises or laughter as they reach an ecstatic high. These manifestations are called 'Kriyas'. Devotees sometimes roar like lions and show all kinds of physical signs during this period. Often devotees move on to higher states of spiritual consciousness and become inert physically and appear to slip into an unconsciousness when they lose sense of what is happening around them. This state is called 'samadhi' and it leads to a deeper spiritual experience."

The guru Shri Yogānandji Mahārāja wrote:

"When Your body begins trembling, hair stands on roots, you laugh or begin to weep without your wishing, your tongue begins to utter deformed sounds, you are filled with fear or see frightening visions... the Kundalini Shakti has become active."

In China there is a popular Kundalini-type movement called 'Qigong'. When Yan Xin, a Chinese Qigong spiritual Master, gave a talk to a crowd in San Francisco in 1991, the San Francisco Chronicle reported that many in the crowd began to experience what Yan called "spontaneous movements". He told his audience, "Those who are sensitive might start having some strong physical sensations – or start laughing or crying. Don't worry. This is quite normal."

Now, doesn't a lot of this sound awfully familiar? Isn't it virtually identical to what we have seen in the church over the last 20 years or so? An empowered leader touching people on the head and all these weird manifestations occurring?

The fact is, in the modern Charismatic movement all this is relatively "new" – having flooded in on a mass level only 20 years ago. There had always been a certain amount of strange goings-on

21

around the "fringes" of the Charismatic scene, but basically it was a fairly sound Bible-based movement for years before all of this. The deluge only started around 1994. So where did it come from – and what 'spirit' was it of?

Please compare the below account from a modern 'revival' with the 'Kundalini' manifestations above. One of my readers sent this to me some years ago – but it is very typical of what many have experienced:

"I inadvertently got prayed over by some people who had received "The Toronto Blessing". I ended up that night with uncontrollable flopping and shaking of my limbs, being drunk in spirit and uncontrollable laughter. At the time it felt right. But later as time went on, these manifestations came at inopportune times and were uncontrollable. My arms and legs would shake when trying to pray for people or when just sitting in church. My legs would give out and I would have to catch my balance just to stand upright while worshipping. It soon became clear to me that this was not the Holy Spirit and so I repented of allowing myself to receive this spirit and asked God to take it away from me. Praise Him, He did!"

Now there is no doubt that a Hindu Guru would describe the above as a 'Kundalini Awakening'. It is virtually identical in every respect. And yet we in the church called it a Blessing from God! And seemingly this same anointing continues to spread via "impartation" meetings all over the world today. Isn't that basically what is happening? Aren't the similarities too obvious to deny?

THE FRANZ MESMER CONNECTION

In the eighteenth century there arose a famous occultic healer named Franz Mesmer – a physician and astrologer born in Germany. Mesmer was the inventor of what he called "animal magnetism" (otherwise known as 'Mesmerism') which was the forerunner of modern Hypnotism. He actually had a kind of occultic "ministry" or healing practice which attracted many of the most prominent figures of European society. And what were the "manifestations" that often resulted? They are described as: "falling down, jerking, convulsions, strange grunts and cries, hysterical laughter, etc." Hmmm. Why do we keep seeing these same recurring manifestations – right through the occult world? Doesn't it seem likely that similar spirits are at work?

As I wrote in that early "Toronto" article:

"To me it seems beyond dispute that there has been a powerful alien spirit let loose in many churches for some considerable time. Just because the Toronto manifestations have been cloaked in "Christian" terminology does not mean that they are from God. The fact is that such manifestations are found nowhere in the Bible, but rather right through the New Age movement. Surely this fact alone should have rung alarm bells?"

MORE "KUNDALINI" TESTIMONIES

In the Hindu religion, Kundalini is usually spoken of as a 'serpent' force positioned in the spine. A 'Kundalini Awakening' is also related to the opening up of the 'chakras' and the opening of the "third eye" in the forehead, etc. As one former New Ager named Peter Bell wrote to me:

" *Before I was gloriously saved and filled with the Holy Spirit (in my early 20s), I was 'experimenting' with a lot of stuff on the streets, including several varieties of New Age spirituality. One of the ones that was presented most powerfully was a system that promoted this Kundalini spirit. The claim was made that this is really just you yourself, your soul or psychic energy, but it was presented in such a way that it included all the nerves of the body, from the base of the spine all the way up to the head. The various energy centers (nerve centers) along the spine were identified as spiritual centers, as in a lot of the Eastern teaching.*

The Kundalini itself is presented as a serpent, the size and shape of the spine, but alive and "entering" or "possessing" the physical body through the nervous system. Depending on how deeply a

23

person has accepted this teaching, the Kundalini spirit could have access to cling to or oppress or even possess a person, telling them the lie that this was really themselves, and leaving them under its control and unable to separate themselves from what is really an alien spirit, far from being their own self or soul."

When our ministry went worldwide on the Internet, a lot of people began to get in touch with us from all over the globe regarding the Toronto/ "River" revival and the manifestations that they were seeing or experiencing. Below are several of these testimonies that we have received over the years:

SHERIE wrote:

" I can testify that I was infested with this foul eastern spirit, the kundalini. I was in a movement from 1992 - 2000 which had close links with the Toronto movement. From 2000 - 2006 I joined a church with links to Bill Johnson.

I was desperate for God to move in my life and change situations and heal hurts and was very open to ministry - I had many in this movement touch my forehead and experienced the manifestations you describe - drunkenness, laughing and crying, shaking. I got dreams and visions and just before I left the structure (church) I had a vivid dream of a huge python that came through the back door and attached itself to my car, and also to rooms in my home. I was very disturbed and sought the Lord for an answer.

It took about 6 months before I was delivered, but God brought a couple over my path who God had trained and had victory over spiritual entities. Every time I was in their presence, I would get very anxious, and they would calmly pray for me and I could feel darkness leaving and my sanity restored. It was only after 6 months of these episodes, I was again in their presence and sensed a fight ensue in the spirit. I was very anxious and fearful and could feel a huge snake in my spine - I was rigid and very uncomfortable - It felt as if this thing wanted to throttle me and rob me of my life. I called out to God and they quietly prayed - then I asked the lady to pull this serpent out of my head - it felt as if it could exit near the top of my crown. She continued to pray and I got the word "kundalini" in my spirit and just commanded this thing by its name to go in the mighty name of Jesus Christ. I pled the blood as it was very frightening, and it left. I felt like a washed out rag, but I was free!

That was the last lime I had deliverance and my spiritual eyes have since opened and God has done a mighty work in me outside of the structure... Afterwards they were amazed and asked me what strange term I had used and where it came from - I had no idea except that it was God who gave me knowledge in that situation. Thank you for the info that has made everything clear to me! I now have confirmation from where I was infected! May many of your readers heed the call of God to "come out and sever yourselves" from Babylon and its lies and deception and foul spirits, while there is time... "

GERI MCGHEE (a deliverance minister) wrote:

I received the following email from a child of God who has been victimized by "soaking" in what she was told was the Holy Spirit. Perhaps, there are others of you who are being tormented after an experience with what you thought was the Holy Spirit; when in reality, you were taken captive by a demonic spirit(s)...

"Dear Geri: I remember going to some meetings where they believed in all of this that you have mentioned in your message on "soaking". I have experienced the shaking, tingling, electrical sensation going through my body, along with various other things that they said was the Holy Spirit, not realizing that it is the Kundalini spirit... Have you ever delivered anyone from this horrible spirit and is it hard?

I have the cold sensations over my head, tingling, electrical sensations going through my body, I can feel a serpent like movement all over my back, I have this shaking when I pray, I feel movement over my head, genitals, legs, etc, the list goes on and on.

25

You may share my testimony because I have struggled with this for many years and no one has been able to help me. I have done some research on this spirit, and what I have found is the very same thing that you have told me. I just recently visited a church where they brought back the impartation of TODD BENTLEY and passed it on to some people including me, not knowing what I was getting into. All of these manifestations are present at his services as well. I can feel it in my chest, on my back and it is a horrible crawling serpent sensation..."

'REVIVAL-FIRE' wrote:

I have a recent testimony of deliverance that may be helpful to some people. In 2003 I ended up in a Toronto Blessing type meeting, I was a youth worker for a Christian organisation at the time. I had some spiritual experiences during this season at the Toronto type church. Something was transferred to me during this time. How do I know?

During this season God had begun to work in the lives of the young people I had been ministering to... After my Toronto meetings, when I now shared at the youth groups, spiritual phenomena began to take place. Laughter broke out, some felt drunk, others would feel like slumping on the floor when I prayed. At the time I didn't understand it, some of it concerned me, but I didn't want to quench it if it was God. One thing that did concern me was that one of the young people who got 'drunkenness' for a couple of days, wasn't even saved.

Anyway, I've always had a love for the word of God, good doctrine and truth. Some of the things in the Toronto stuff never sat right with me. I did think there where some New Age influences. I did relax on the manifestations though and I have laughed, shook, jerked and 'whoooooaaaaahhhhhed' with the best of them. Since that point I was a defender of 'Toronto'...

Having had hands laid on me by many Toronto people I began to wonder about impartation and what I had received. One day while out in the town some American Indians where doing some of their Native Music on the streets. I stopped to listen and as I listened I began to feel movement in my gut. The movement I felt was very similar to what I would feel during times of 'praise and worship'. I thought to myself, Why is my spirit being moved (in an enjoyable way) by this pagan music? At this point I began to wonder about what sort of spirits I had opened myself up to.

Anyway, the 'new mystics' meeting that I ended up at last week (I didn't know that is who they were) caused me to still feel that something wasn't right. Although my eyes had been opened to the deception, I still felt there was still a spiritual tie. I say this because my 'spirit' would respond to what was happening in the meeting at times even though it was obviously chaotic. Also during worship some people came up while I was worshipping and prayed for me. Again I felt that this wasn't good.

The few days that followed this meeting were pretty awful emotionally. I felt drained, down and depressed. I then remembered that this is how I would often feel when I would come out of the Toronto meetings. In those days I would interpret this as God bringing negative stuff to the surface to deal with things. However as this began to happen again I began to doubt that this was the case. I also found it hard to pray and read the word.

Anyway, while in bed, a few nights later, my wife was led to begin to pray for me. As she was praying while laying hands on my stomach she saw 'a little black thing'. However she noticed that the little black thing was held tight and gripped by a fist. As she prayed it left. She did not tell me this until the morning.

After she had prayed I felt better, went to sleep and woke up the next day much lighter. She then told me what she had seen. How I interpret it is like this: Through the laying on of hands and opening myself up to a deception the enemy had got access.

Recent events caused me to see the truth of the deception regarding the spirit at work, my eyes where opened but there was still a spiritual tie on the inside (probably due to transference). The fact that it was held tight by a fist caused me to believe that the spirit had been 'bound' but that I had not been delivered. Perhaps this binding of the spirit is what has caused me to see the truth, however deliverance did not come until my wife prayed. Anyway, ever since this experience I have found that a lot of 'things' have 'lifted off me'.

DEBYLYNNE wrote:

'Revival-fire' - I found your post very interesting, especially when you talked about the "responses" you would feel and sense in yourself to things that you knew were not of God (ie. Indian music) and how similar they were to what you "felt" in response to "god" in these services. I have had the same experiences and it has really troubled me. Even when I was watching the clips about the Kundalini and I would "feel" myself begin to respond and "jerk" and "twitch" and shake and I would turn it off immediately because that rather "freaked me out". I have never been to Toronto, nor have I had "direct" contact with anyone that has been there - but I have watched the stuff on God TV and I have "laid hands" on the TV screen to "receive" and I thought it was ALL of God.

I have repented wholeheartedly, but I wonder if there is still something on the inside of me that needs stronger action taken against it. I have not had my husband pray for me concerning this, but I believe that I WILL..."

BRENDA writes:

A very dear friend of mine who has been my prayer partner for years was lured into the enemy's web of deception about many of the ministries and manifestations that you spoke about. After reading and listening to your web broadcasts we had a powerful prayer session repenting, renouncing, and commanding any spirit that we had picked up from these false prophets/doctrines of demons, etc. to go from us in Jesus' name. We broke all kinds of things off of us. Most of it was deep repentance and renouncing –

thank you for exposing the enemy and his tactics and all the deception that the church body has fallen deeply into...

HOW TO GET FREE

Yes - if you have had "hands laid" or done "soaking prayer" under any of these kinds of ministries, it is very important to RENOUNCE (from the very depths of your being in Jesus' name) and also COMMAND OUT these Kundalini spirits or any other "anointings" that you have received. Remember, the whole idea is to "violently expel" these things in the name of Jesus Christ. Be SET FREE in His mighty name!

It is vital to understand that every true believer has God-given authority to establish God's rule over the "territory" inside of them, so-to-speak. While it is important to deeply REPENT before God with true "godly sorrow" if you have opened yourself up to these spirits, it is also vital to know that you can COMMAND these things to go in the name of Jesus Christ! I often talk about "RENOUNCING" things from the very depths of your being. It is not just with your 'mouth only'. You are to use the "Sword of the Spirit." You are to reject and expel these things with every part of you - spirit, soul and body - in the mighty name of Jesus Christ. And they WILL go! Stop being "passive" about it. You need to get aggressive with these things!

The same applies to other areas of darkness in people's lives. If you suffer from depression or a bad temper or any other form of darkness that you can't seem to get rid of – COMMAND it gone from the very depths of your being in Jesus' name! I refer to many of these things as "strongholds" rather than 'demons'. And I have seen people utterly delivered of things they thought were "ingrained" in them - just by deeply and utterly COMMANDING them gone in the mighty name of Jesus. "The weapons of our warfare are not carnal, but mighty through God to the pulling down of strongholds" (2 Cor 10:4).

GOD'S HOLY CHARACTER

Another key thing that I pointed out in my original Toronto article was that a lot of this type of deception arises out of a false understanding of "WHO GOD IS" – and His character. Our very view of God and His personality can either set us up for deception – or protect us from it. And the exact same principle applies to discerning the ministries of men like Todd Bentley and John Crowder today. As I wrote in 1996:

" *On the one hand we have Toronto's version of "God" - a being who lives to bring `touches' and bodily sensations upon his people, who loves to "party" with them - to `loosen them up' so that they cast off all restraint and do foolish things that they would never normally do. Many of these touches may appear to outside observers to be `ugly' or even revolting and frightening (similar to asylum-type mental or drug disorders, etc), but, hey, let's just get our mind out of the way, relax and enjoy it all! Who cares if it looks or sounds completely 'demonic' (animal noises, hysterical laughter, bizarre jerking, etc), so long as it feels good and seems to heal all those past 'hurts'? To me, this is the very essence of the touchy-feely "Laodicean" view of God – a 'God' made entirely in their own image, and for their own convenience. Love without responsibility. Mercy without judgment. A permissive, "Santa Claus" God - perfect for the shallow, pleasure-loving age in which we live.* "

If you have a false understanding of "WHO GOD IS" then I strongly urge you to repent, my friends. If your God is not a Holy God, but rather a "party" God or a big "Blessing" sugar-daddy in the sky – then you will open yourself up to deception time and time again. We have got to get our concept of "Who God is" right – in order to avoid deadly spiritual seduction in these last days.

CHAPTER THREE

EYEWITNESS WARNINGS

We stated earlier in this book that there are strong linkages between ministries and movements such as Rodney Howard-Browne, the Toronto blessing, the Prophetic movement, the Lakeland revival, Todd Bentley, John Crowder, etc. And hopefully you saw confirmation of this in the previous chapter. For years now people have been experiencing the exact same types of "manifestations" throughout these different circles. And that is because it is the exact same "anointing" – the exact same spirit.

As I said, I am familiar with these linkages because I was part of the Prophetic movement for 11 years. But I was also fighting a "rearguard action" that entire time, trying to keep a lot of this junk out (and mostly failing). I was very aware of where it was coming from, and who was carrying it. And I want to tell you – the years 1994 to 1998 were a very difficult and tumultuous time for our ministry because of this.

During 1996 and 1997 in particular I was literally bombarded with more and more angry emails from leaders and Christians around the world trying to get me to back down. And it got even worse when we published our first articles on the Brownsville revival. It was staggering – the uproar that ensued!

What we have to realize is that Toronto was a very "contagious" anointing. It literally spread everywhere – simply by the laying on of hands. In England during those years, the two most prominent centers for "imparting" this anointing seemed to be Sunderland Christian Centre under the ministry of Ken and Lois Gott, and Holy Trinity Brompton under the ministry of Sandy Millar. Both places had got their 'anointing' directly from Toronto. But now it was about to spread into an entirely new fold altogether.

BROWNSVILLE – THE NEXT BIG THING

The revival in Brownsville, Pensacola was a bit of an enigma in some ways. It was centered in an Assembly of God church. And, unlike Toronto itself, Brownsville definitely involved real Repentance preaching, due to the involvement of men like Steve Hill and Dr. Michael Brown – who had been holiness and repentance preachers for years before that time. (I guess the AOG may not have accepted this move without that). However, there is no question that the Toronto spirit was given a huge place there also – right from the start.

June 18, 1995 was the day that the Brownsville revival officially broke out. Yet despite the real repentance that was prominent at times, "Toronto" was also an enormous factor. And they didn't even really try to hide it.

Speaking of the "manifestations" that were going on in their midst, the Brownsville pastor John Kilpatrick himself described them as: *"Falling on the floor… physical healing, receiving of visions, feeling the love of God, Laughter, Shaking of head, hands, feet and body; Deep bowing."*

Can anybody tell any real difference between the Toronto manifestations and the ones described at Brownsville? The answer is "No," because there is no real difference. It was only the repentance preaching that truly set Brownsville apart. So it seemed to be a kind-of "mixture".

When Steve Beard from Good News Magazine interviewed Steve Hill, the main preacher at Brownsville, he asked him how he had come to end up at Holy Trinity Brompton – the big 'Toronto' church in London – just before going to Brownsville. Steve Hill didn't even try to hide anything. He replied:

"... they were laughing, they were falling, and I had a very critical spirit... I walked into the stately Anglican church in downtown London right by Harrod's, the richest area of town, and stepped over about 500 bodies, people shaking all over the place... The Lord spoke to my heart and said, "You don't need to talk to Sandy Miller. Just have him pray for you... I went up to him, he laid his hands on my head and it was over. I mean, I went down under the power..."

So there it is! That's how Steve Hill caught this 'anointing'! And clearly he transferred it straight into Brownsville when he went there soon after. Given that both John Kilpatrick and Steve Hill openly admitted this strong "Toronto-ish" influence at Brownsville, you would think that there would have been no disputing it. But you should have seen the firestorm when I wrote my first article on the subject!

It was simply called, "Brownsville, Pensacola – Toronto or Not?" But one thing I should have done that would have given the article more balance, was to strongly commend the Repentance preaching that was taking place – because it is a fact that many people who visited Brownsville were deeply convicted by the preaching and truly repented of their sins. I should have acknowledged this far more vocally than I did. But I was too concerned with the Kundalini invasion that was seemingly going up another gear.

That is why today I call Brownsville an "enigma." It was like a mixture of both things – the good and the bad. And sometimes it was very difficult to work out which side was 'winning'. Let me give you an example. In late April 1997 I received the following email written by a woman who was confirmed as one of the major prayer leaders at Brownsville. This email was being enthusiastically distributed by a PRO-PENSACOLA Email List:

Hope these latest reports from Brownsville thrill you as much as they do me! – Jim W.

From: Cathie W.

Written to a friend about the Gott's visit to Brownsville

Dear Cathleen,

You asked me what's up.... so....... here goes!

The Gott's (Ken and Lois) from Sunderland England are here.. for conference at Brownsville. (Mrs. Kilpatrick just got home from their church also...)

Well... they seem to have an impartation for intercession and going a bit deeper in the river...!!!

They prayed for the prayer team last night for about 45 min. before church. It was such a strong anointing. The room was full of everyone of us behaving as if electricity was charging thru us in huge waves. Uncontrollable yells were coming out of us... As a matter of fact... Ouch.. they are hitting me as I try to describe it. My head keeps getting swallowed up by my shoulders in huge jerks as "OHHHH!" comes out of my mouth as if my voice and body are synchronized. Last night... my head seemed to get so much lower than my shoulders that at one point, my head was in my blouse.. ha ha ha ha ha.. I am starting to laugh now.......................

whoa............... Oops... there I go again!

Some time between 6:15 and 7:00 my earrings broke off... Who knows how or when???? Maybe My shoulders did it!!!...

Well, after those prayers last night, we were manifesting like we did in the beginning.. only louder. Trying to walk was harder. Going in a straight line and completely upright was nearly impossible for the whole night. Staying silent was also nearly impossible. The OH's came without thought or fore-knowledge that it was about to come.

I was assigned to pray in the Chapel last night... The Spirit seemed to rush right through the person being prayed for and hit the catcher too. My knees kept giving out and I'd end up in a squatting position going "OHHHHHHHHH!"

I got Pastor S-- from another AOG to pray for me. As he turned toward me.. I started deep bowing until he touched my head and then I went electric until I crashed to the floor. My head was trying to hide in my blouse again.. ha ha ha ha .. my pockets emptied.. my tags and certs were everywhere. I could see them but I couldn't get them. Some people around me tried to help me up but it was no use... My legs would not hold me up. I don't know how long I was down but when the lights started going out (Sweet Elmer strikes again!) I made myself get up and wobbled in a bent over position all the way to the car. I did the OHHH's all the way. No one pays any attention to people like me anymore.. its a common sight here but for a prayer team member.. who can manage a lot of anointing, its a bit unusual to be so overcome. I had to set my cruise control on the car to 35mph or else I would find myself slowing down to 20 mph as I boxed the air in intercession all the way home...

I dreamed of being at church while I slept. Jerks woke me up several times. It was very nice. When I got to the lab this morning and picked up some photos of the Gott's praying for some others the day before... I start the bowing and had to stop looking at them in public!!! Instead of the loud OHH'S.. I had some more quiet EWE'S.. ha ha ha ha... that poor Lab....they know me by now!!! I will write about the Banner service and Golden Altar service later.. but since you asked what was UP... I just had to tell you while this is so fresh!

As I said, the above email was confirmed as being written by a recognized Prayer Leader at Brownsville. I hope you can see why I was so concerned about the 'spirit' that was being "imparted" there – because believers from all over the world were rushing to Pensacola to bring this anointing back to their own church. I felt I had no choice but to speak out for the sake of the precious sheep – and to do so in the most urgent terms.

By this time we were no longer quite the "little guys" at the bottom of the world that everybody ignored. We were still small, but we had a lot of people forwarding our material all over the world. Even Dr. Michael Brown himself felt that he had to write articles specifically against the things that we were saying. The pressure from around the globe to compromise and back down was intense. But when I truly looked at the FACTS and the quotes from the leaders' OWN MOUTHS, I simply realized that we could never stop our warnings. There was indeed an "invasion" going on, and come what may, it was important for us to stand our ground. But those were difficult and pressure-filled days.

Naturally the main thing we were accused of was being 'judgmental' or "religious". Many called us 'Accusers of the brethren,' and other awful things. After months and months of this, it can begin to wear on you. But how can you back off in such a situation? What happens to the precious sheep if no-one warns them any more of imminent danger? Didn't Jesus and the apostles publicly warn about certain ministries in their day – because of the danger to the sheep? Are we supposed to just shut our mouths and let alien spirits deceive and destroy the church? Aren't we commanded in Scripture to sound the alarm to the Body if we see such things occurring? We did not WANT to become known as the "negative nay-sayers" – but tell me, what choice did we have?

THE SICK GETS SICKER

I hope it is starting to become clear exactly where the "drunken" antics of men like Todd Bentley and John Crowder come from. All of that started way back with Rodney Howard-Browne and the Toronto blessing. These guys are simply "children of the revolution." But just in case you have not yet fully grasped how close these linkages and 'spirits' are, here is something that simply adds sickness upon sickness to what we have already seen. It is called the "New Wine Drinking Song" – and was put out some years ago by a couple very prominent in the Toronto movement – Richard and Kathryn Riss. Below are extracts from the email that they sent out on the 'New Wine' List promoting it:

Dear New Winos:

I am not a songwriter, neither the son of a songwriter, but the Lord gave me a "New Winos Drinking Song Number One". You can sing it to the tune of "Tis the Gift to be Simple" or "When the Roll is Called Up Yonder". See if it makes you as drunk as it makes me! It goes like this...

Now I'm just a party animal grazing at God's trough,

I'm a Jesus junkie, and I can't get enough!

I'm an alcoholic for that great New Wine,

'Cause the Holy Ghost is pouring, and I'm drinking all the time!

Now I laugh like an idiot and bark like a dog,

If I don't sober up, I'll likely hop like a frog!

And I'll crow like a rooster 'til the break of day,

'Cause the Holy Ghost is moving, and I can't stay away!

Now I roar like a lioness who's on the prowl,

I laugh and I shake, maybe hoot like an owl!

Since God's holy river started bubbling up in me,

It spills outside, and it's setting me free!

So, I'll crunch and I'll dip and I'll dance round and round,

'Cause the pew was fine, but it's more fun on the ground!

So I'll jump like a pogo stick, then fall on the floor,

'Cause the Holy Ghost is moving, and I just want MORE!...

Somebody asked me for permission to "use it." I told the Lord if He ever gave me any music, I would give it away. So, the rules I just made up for "using it" are:

1. Everybody sing it as much as you want and get as drunk as you can! Just thinking about it gives me holy laughter. I taught the Jesus Junkie verse (it was all I could get out from laughing so hard) to our little prayer group last night, and they all got pretty sloshed, for Presbyterians. Especially since the guy who was supposed to bring his guitar came late, without it, so the only other music we sang all evening was "Happy Birthday to You." A capella.

2. Pass it on to as many other New Winos as you want...

Blessings! Kathryn Riss.

I guess we could be accused at this point of poking fingers at someone else's "fun." After all, it seems pretty harmless and silly getting into the kind of spiritual 'drunkenness' described above. However, the big problem is that the self-same "anointing" that produces all this drunkenness and foolishness is the same spirit that gets people loaded with Kundalini. This is simply one aspect of that self-same spirit – just like the jerking, the laughter, the convulsions and the 'serpent' sensations, etc. It all comes from the same source.

After more than 15 years, I think it is now possible to see what utterly sick and destructive fruit this spirit has produced in the long-term (though of course, it seemed great 'fun' at the start).

Paul Gowdy, a former Vineyard pastor from the Toronto area, made the following observations years later:

"After three years of being in the thick of the Toronto blessing our Vineyard assembly in Scarborough (East Toronto) just about self destructed. We devoured one another, with gossip, backstabbing, division, sects, criticism, etc. After three years of 'soaking,' praying for people, shaking, rolling, laughing, roaring, ministering at TACF on their prayer team, leading worship at TACF, preaching at TACF, basically living at TACF - we were the most carnal, immature and deceived Christians that I know. I remember saying to my friend and senior pastor at Scarborough Vineyard Church in 1997 that ever since the Toronto Blessing came we have just about fallen to bits! He agreed!

My experience has been that the manifestation of spiritual gifts mentioned in 1st Corinthians 12 was much more common in our assembly before January 1994 (when the Toronto blessing started) than during this period of supposed Holy Spirit visitation.

During 1992-1993 when praying for people we would experience what I believe was genuine prophecy, deliverance and much grace and favour from the Lord. After the Toronto Blessing started, all ministry time changed, the only prayers were 'More, Lord, MORE', the shouting of 'Fire', the jerky shaking of the body with the 'ooh ooh OOH WOOOAAH' prayer. (I kid you not!)..."

It doesn't sound like Paul Gowdy considers the long-term fruit of Toronto to be much other than "bad". And I have to concur. In fact, I believe that this 'spirit' has left a trail of destruction through the Body of Christ in the last 20 years that is almost beyond comprehension. Furthermore, I believe we would be struggling to come up with anything in the entire history of the church that has created more chaos. One would almost think that it was "judgment" – beginning in the house of God.

CASTAWAYS AND PARIAHS

Even today when I reflect back on this era in the 1990s, I can't help thinking what "might have been." This whole period had been preceded by a lot of prayer for real Revival, and a lot of expectation that God was truly going to move. But when these counterfeits flooded in, it was almost as though they swept up all of those prayers and all of that expectancy – into a movement that consisted of little more than froth and foolishness. The Charismatic movement to this day has never recovered.

Speaking personally, I had a good idea that I was literally flushing my whole preaching ministry straight down the toilet by speaking out on these issues. I knew I would most likely never be asked to preach or minister anywhere that any of these 'big names' had any influence. I was making myself into a complete pariah. And so I had to count the cost.

I sometimes ask myself the question, even now. If I had to do it over again, would I make the same choices – and oppose those things so vocally? And I have to conclude – the answer is 'Yes.' If I had to do it over again, I would do it mostly the same. Maybe even "louder"! For if we do not warn when something very damaging is afflicting the Body of Christ, what kind of servant are we?

People are often surprised when they hear me preach, for I usually do not major on the topic of 'deception'. The thing that I feel truly called and anointed to preach is Repentance – and the experience of a truly "clean heart" before God. That is where I really see results. But there is no doubt that I am a "pariah" still, in many circles. And it does cause me sadness to think that the message God gave me will likely never be heard for the most part. But yes – I would do things and say things mostly the same if I had my time over again.

DID 'PROSPERITY' OPEN THE DOOR?

Several Spirit-filled leaders, who were on the front lines when this invasion flooded in, have wondered what may have opened the door for it to enter the church. In my view, there were a couple of factors. One major candidate is the "Prosperity gospel" of the 1970s and 1980s – for though there was some opposition to it in Charismatic circles, the outcry was not nearly large enough. And slowly this false doctrine began to dominate the movement more and more. It was this spirit of compromise – with something that was clearly error – that I believe may have been a key allowing Toronto to invade in the years to follow.

Another open door, in my view, was that leaders in the Vineyard and the Prophetic movement (which were very influential at the time) were becoming desperate for "something" to happen. And they were willing to settle for the 'quick and easy' counterfeit, rather than waiting for the real thing. They opted for the Ishmael, rather than waiting for the Isaac. And all of us have been paying the price, ever since.

CHAPTER FOUR

INVASION OF THE PROPHETIC

A lot of people, when they find out how many years I remained within the ranks of the Prophetic movement, can't understand why I didn't leave a lot earlier. They ask me, "Couldn't you see how deceived it was?" The answer is, "Yes, I could!" (I've just been laying out how bad things were!) But I felt for a long time that by staying involved with it and calling for a return to the original principles and the original call over that movement, something could still be salvaged.

You have to realize that the modern Prophetic movement was not always like it is today. The reason I was drawn to it in the first place was that originally – in its earliest days – this was a movement concerned with holiness, intercession and true Revival.

It had always seemed very significant to me that when the modern 'Prophetic' was beginning in Kansas City in 1982, God very clearly spoke to the leadership, saying that it was to be built on "four standards" - which were: (1) Night and day prayer; (2) Holiness of heart; (3) Unwavering faith; and (4) Extravagant giving to the poor. Another predominant word from the Lord to the movement right at the beginning was: "I am going to change the understanding and expression of Christianity IN THE EARTH in one generation."

Now, just imagine if the modern Prophetic had actually made a real stand, loudly and boldly proclaiming these "four standards" to the church right through the 1980's. Imagine if they had used their notoriety to preach "Night & day prayer, holiness of heart, unwavering faith, and extravagant giving to the poor." Imagine if THAT was the message they became known for!

But no. Instead they became known for flaky teachings, fallen prophets and bizarre "manifestations". There was quite a purity about those early days in the 1980's, which seemed to last for only a few years. But slowly the whole thing became infiltrated, and ended up becoming a terrible spiritual quagmire.

Is it not possible that God wanted to raise up a prophetic voice in those days to call the Laodicean church to repentance before it was too late? (There were prophecies about this at the time). I believe this is very possible, but it is not what happened. In fact, the 1980's turned out to be the "tipping point" for excess and greed flooding into the church - and particularly into the Charismatic movement. These were the years that the Prosperity doctrine made vast inroads, and televangelists began to bring the name of Christ into greater and greater reproach.

Imagine if there had been a real Prophetic movement to "cry aloud and spare not" during that time. The history of the church right up to our own day might have been vastly different. But it was not to be.

The Prophetic movement was never supposed to be dominated by 'revelatory' experiences or spectacular dreams and visions. It was not supposed to be about selling books or holding conferences. It was supposed to bring a word that would shake the church out of her slumber - that would pierce her heart with 'godly sorrow' and deep repentance before it was too late. It was supposed to bring great shaking and change - to act as a 'John-the-Baptist' to the nation.

But then came the 'invasion' – and destroyed what little remained.

THE KANSAS CITY PROPHETS

By the time Toronto hit in 1994, the Kansas City Prophetic movement was already in serious trouble – and had already lost a great deal that it had in the beginning. The movement was led in Kansas City by Mike Bickle – not a "prophet" himself, but more of an intercessor and pastor. The movement had begun with a great deal of prayer in the 1980's, but was now being driven into deep deception by the enemy. And Toronto would be the final straw. The 'Prophetic' would never be the same again.

So did this Kansas City movement support the "invasion"? You bet! They fell for it, hook, line and sinker. As I said, they had been prophesying, "Revival, Revival" for so long that they were getting rather desperate by this time. And so they seemingly fell for the first "power" move that came along – whether it was counterfeit or not. In fact, they became some of its biggest proponents.

A lot of people who support Mike Bickle's ministry today do not realize that in one of his most popular books, 'Growing in the Prophetic,' he has an entire section where he defends Toronto and the strange manifestations that were occurring. It is also a fact that when the main 'Toronto' church was expelled from the Vineyard movement in late 1995, Mike Bickle took his own church out of the Vineyard "in sympathy". It was during those years that the Prophetic and Toronto became almost "one movement". You would commonly see big Prophetic conferences where leaders from the Toronto/ 'River' movement would be sharing the stage with the big "prophets". All of this became commonplace. And no surprise that soon Prophetic meetings around the world started to resemble the same kind of "menagerie" that we were seeing in Toronto.

I don't know if you have ever ministered in a church where the pastor jerks his head suddenly every few moments when he talks, and emits a little 'yelp'. Yes, I have preached in a church like that. Or I don't know if you have been in meetings where you almost felt like you were in a Zoo - because so many strange 'manifestations' were occurring all over the room. Yes, I have been in those too.

It very quickly got to the point where the Prophetic movement became almost the main "carrier" and proponent of 'Toronto'. And as they merged into one, the "peer pressure" became almost unbearable. If you didn't go along with it, you were in trouble.

But still we found we simply could not back down. Every ounce of discernment within me was screaming that this was the "counterfeit" that was sweeping through before the real Revival. I felt it was a 'test' - to see if the prophets truly were "lovers of truth" and also to see if they could be trusted to lead thousands of young converts in a full-blown Revival. There is no doubt in my mind that the Prophetic movement miserably failed this test. And it has led directly to all the flakiness that we see today. This is where it really comes from.

Suddenly the most wild things were occurring - and being completely accepted as being "from God". People were manifesting in such a way that clearly would have been considered "demonic" before - but was now accepted as somehow being "of the Spirit". It was like a living nightmare. We could hardly believe it. And the pressure to conform was incredible.

Of course, the basic mantra of the whole thing was "not to judge" these things with your mind, but to simply "open yourself up" to them. But isn't this exactly what the New Age teaches? What kind of 'discernment' is that?

Of course when I published my findings on all this I was attacked bitterly – especially from within the Prophetic camp itself (even though I was "one of them," so to speak. In fact, I think that made it worse). They didn't want anyone spoiling the "party". And so the wreckage continued.

The total lack of discernment amongst so many 'prophets' today, the silly and unbiblical practices, etc - so much of it originated in this period. There is actually a kind "blindness" that develops. For if someone persists in 'believing a lie' then eventually they will be given over to it. And this is even more true of prophets. For prophets are supposed to LOVE THE TRUTH.

TORONTO AS A "TEST"

As I said, I am convinced that basically this movement was a 'test' for the church. A Spirit-filled preacher named Royal Cronquist made the following comments:

This concerns the so-called "Laughing Revival" which began in Toronto, Canada, and spread throughout the nations. In all the meetings I attended, I had the sensation of embarrassment, then shame, finally leaving each meeting grieved in my inner man. I never made a final judgment, because I had to seek the Lord in prayer concerning all the negative sensing going on within me...

Later, Jesus appeared to me in my room and what He said overwhelmed, shocked and surprised me: "The manifestations presently going on in the laughing revival have happened to varying degrees with every outpouring of the Holy Spirit. But in this one, we gave great liberty to Satan, commissioning him to initiate and do as he willed...

"We wanted to put Our people, especially Church leaders, to the test to see if they would "try the spirits" to see whether they were of God or not (1 JN 4:1); to examine everything and hold fast to that which was good, and ensure that everything glorified the Godhead in attitude, motive, word or deed (1 TH 5:21); to see if the leaders would hold or keep the meetings in decency and order (1 CO 14:40). Even many of the blessings and apparent miracles came from the source of Satan with Our consent."

Church leaders miserably failed the test. Why? Because they have failed to seek the counsel of the Most High (JE 23:16-22). Therefore, in the Day of the Lord, because they have refused to grow up into Me in all aspects, I will give them over to their own lusts. I will give them a spirit of delusion whereby they will believe lies (2 TH 2:10b-11; RE 13:14a)...

There is nothing worse than being "given over to believe a lie" by God – simply because you have been chasing after 'power' and experiences so much that you are willing to fall for anything. In my opinion, being "given over" like that is the ultimate form of deception. It is a fate that I would not wish on anyone. So did this happen with 'Toronto'? Sadly I have to conclude that – yes, it did. There was a very "strong delusion" involved in all of this. And we saw it again later when Lakeland came along. The same blindness, the same deluded mindset among leaders. It was truly astounding.

I have studied church history long enough to know that there has never been a 'Kundalini invasion' of the church on a worldwide scale like this before. The last 20 years have seen something that I believe has never occurred anywhere else in history – a massive invasion by deceiving spirits of a size and scope to boggle the mind. But I believe that God Himself will have the final say.

WHO WERE THE KC PROPHETS?

There is no question that the main Kansas City prophet right through the early years was Bob Jones. It is very difficult to pinpoint when he began to go astray into deception, but I believe it was a gradual process. In 1992, after something of a scandal, he left KC to become involved with Rick Joyner's ministry in North Carolina. Sadly, I believe his ministry became more and more polluted. He prophesied all kinds of grand things over Lakeland before it came crashing down – and generally stood behind much of the flakiness that goes on in Prophetic circles today. He was a big supporter of the Kundalini invasion, and his influence seemed to permeate the whole prophetic scene.

To give you some idea, here is a transcript of some of the comments that Bob Jones made to Todd Bentley on stage at Lakeland:

BOB: "I released my angels to him... this man from Canada asked for my angels; this Wind of Change is most powerful. Except for the arch angels, this 'Winds of Change', this is the most powerful angel..."

BOB TO TODD BENTLEY: "As I watch you, you VIBRATE. You know there are two portals, clockwise and counter-clockwise. When you vibrate you close demonic vibration. Counter-clockwise *vibration is demonic. The vibration is healing. Does it seem peculiar?" [He waves his hands]... "I'm releasing it to you."*

I don't know about you, but I cannot see anything remotely biblical about the above comments. But sadly, for many years, Bob Jones was a "mentor" to many of the biggest 'prophets' and Charismatic leaders in the world – including Rick Joyner and others. (Bob Jones passed away in February 2012).

The other well-known "prophets" out of Kansas City were John Paul Jackson (also now deceased), James Goll, and in later years Paul Cain. Again, I believe that all of them came to have ministries that were sadly tainted by false spirits to one degree or another. Of course, very few of these men ministered out of Kansas City any more anyway. It was Rick Joyner's Morningstar Ministries that started to become more and more the "center" of the Prophetic world from the mid-1990's onward.

THINGS GET WEIRDER STILL...

By 1999, the first two big "waves" – Toronto and Brownsville – had finally died down. But the Kundalini invasion was not finished yet – not by a long shot! What happened is that it retreated back into the Prophetic movement, where it could percolate and mutate – ready to leap out and envelop the Charismatic world once again when the opportunity arose. But now things got even stranger than they had ever been before.

These were the years when all kinds of weird and bizarre New Age-type phenomena took over. There came a great obsession with "portals", trances, strange 'angels', gold-dust, gemstones, spiritual drunkenness, orbs of light, drum circles, 'third heaven' visualizations – and every other bizarre thing you can imagine. A lot of Christians honestly couldn't see how "New Age" this was all getting – but surely it was as obvious as it could possibly be! And naturally it was mostly coming from the same deceived crowd that had been into all the previous weirdness. I guess it is like a drug addict. You need a greater and greater "high" to keep you going.

And so the entire movement got further and further off the rails. And along with these bizarre new phenomena came a whole new wave of 'Prophetic' leaders who specialized in such things.

Patricia King was one who became a big name during this period. It's not like she was really "new" – but suddenly she and a host of others came into more and more prominence. Todd Bentley was another one. So were David Herzog and Joshua Mills, Bobby Conner and Paul Keith Davis – and many more.

PROPHETIC WEIRDNESS ABOUNDS

Let me share a testimony to give you some idea of the kinds of dangerous and bizarre spiritual practices that were beginning to dominate this movement. The following account comes from an older woman that I know to be a very dedicated Spirit-filled Christian – a real woman of prayer.

LYNN wrote:

"After receiving the Baptism of the Holy Spirit, God began to do a miracle in my heart and I for the first time in my life understood what real sin was and that it separated you from a Holy God... I was so spiritually hungry for Him. My problem was I began to look for Him in all the wrong places. My first encounter was to sit under the teachings of Jill Austin - and to be taught and prayed over by her and listen to all her angelic visitations. This just opened up more doors to deception and darkness. It is by the grace of God that I was able to come out of this deception - but not right away and without God radically showing me the error in my ways.

I became introduced to the Prophetic Movement because Jill Austin was with the whole Kansas City prophetic movement and I trusted in her judgment - after all she was a Prophetic voice? I started running around to all the big name conferences - even a prayer person in a few - not realizing that I was operating in the flesh and seeing man more than God. There is a huge deception there that satan makes you think you are chasing after God. I have heard all the stories of angels - angel dust - feathers - not realizing

48

that this was just another deception from satan to distract your worship away from God and to put it on experiences - man and angels. However, I did never worship angels - but my focus was on the "Man of God" and how spiritual the Man of God is - and I am telling you, that is exactly what these big-name people live for - they are not millions of dollars rich because they preach the cross and repentance.

There are spirits of darkness that follow most of these big conferences and the Holy Spirit would bring up red flags and allowed me to see this spirit of darkness in two of these big lady conference leaders - even to the point they were screeching - and so I said, Thank you Lord that you have shown me these are false prophets. And so I go looking for the ones who are real - "right!" - still not heeding the small voice of the Holy Spirit within me. - Rodney Howard Brown - and the Holy Spirit still showed me the darkness and spirit he operated in - so I decide to check out Patricia King and Todd Bentley and, ignorant of their Third Heaven guided visualizations, attended a five day conference of Patricia King and then two of Todd Bentley's conferences and began to imagine third heaven visitations - guided visualization - still not realizing that these are actually spirits of darkness - the New Age calls them spirit guides - demons is what they are. And so I bought Todd Bentley's teaching on third heaven visitations and brought it home to listen to.

I was in my living room laying on the floor listening to the teaching on how to visualize the third heaven and what to say and was getting caught up into his teaching and all of a sudden I began to shake uncontrollably and jerk and groan, and no sooner had this taken place I became frozen stiff - I could not move any part of my body and I knew this was a demon trying to take hold of me, and so with all the effort I could muster I cried out, "God save me - Jesus help me" - and as soon as I cried out to the Lord my body went limp. God spared me that night and I will be forever grateful.

I spent much of the night in tears asking God to forgive me - and renouncing all the hands laid on me and all the awful deception I had opened myself up to, and most of all grieving the Holy Spirit within me and setting a horrible example of the true power and person of the Holy Spirit.

So it is very hard for me to be quiet and not sound the alarm when these things come up, for I have been there, done that - several years back - and I will warn and sound the alarm and tell people that many of these walk in spiritual darkness - oh, they bring enough truth to make it seem they are the called true apostles/prophets of God! May many be spared from their deception..."

Another report comes from a young Spirit-filled pastor who attended a Patricia King meeting in Arizona:

PASTOR 'M.S' wrote:

These so-called prophets and worship leaders were ushering in lude and familiar spirits, worshipping angels and opening and going through ungodly spiritual portals. I have never been so grieved and disturbed by anything in my life! And nobody else seemed to notice or care...!

Here is another testimony from someone who was deeply involved in this whole movement for many years:

JACK wrote:

I have been involved in the prophetic movement since probably '98 or so, but had even attended Mike Bickle's church before then... I got into going to Todd Bentley revivals and was to some extent – probably a great extent – deceived by what was going on. I read Patricia King's book 'Spiritual Revolution', Todd Bentley's biography, and Mike Bickle's stuff too, as well as Rick Joyner's stuff. It's dangerous and very deceptive because so much of it actually sounds like or reads like the real, but there is a different spirit there. Maybe I was just deceived because I was so susceptible to it...

I also went to Arizona to see the "Extreme Prophetic" stuff and noticed Joshua Mills at one of the meetings covered in "sapphire dust" – "blue glitter" that had apparently materialized on him as oil came out of his shoes – and they showed people a jar of fragrant oil that smelled like wine that had dripped from his hands earlier. I really was gullible because, "Wow - something was happening out of the ordinary" – it had to be God, I thought. I didn't consider that "an evil and adulterous generation seeks for a sign."

Well, I came back to my hometown and then Lakeland started. I didn't go because I knew God was with me where I was. People became crazed and flew out there. IHOP even had impartation meetings. Then I saw Bentley... take big offerings at Morningstar and then news of his affair and immoral lifestyle hit. Confusion baffled me and then the questions came. I have slowly been climbing out of this ditch filled with deep darkness. Thank you for speaking the truth in love...

If you would, will you please pray for me as the Lord leads, if He does, that He would deliver me from every residue of strong delusion and lead me into the truth, all TRUTH. That I would indeed be delivered from every lie that I have believed, as I hear and believe the TRUTH.

BILL JOHNSON, CHE AHN & CO.

While warning of the more openly "extreme" types of ministries, it is also important to remember that there are others who represent a more "acceptable face" to this movement. Bill Johnson is the pastor of Bethel church in Redding, California, a hugely influential fellowship in the Charismatic movement. Bill is the author of the book, "When Heaven Invades Earth" and says many good things – especially about healing and ministering on the streets, etc. Sadly, behind the scenes, Bethel (and especially their School of Ministry) is literally LOADED with Toronto-type flakiness, spiritual "drunkenness", and so-on. Many of the most extreme ministers of that type of "anointing" are regularly invited to teach and 'impart' at the Bethel School. Bill Johnson himself was one of those who

51

got up on stage at Lakeland to endorse the Todd Bentley revival just before it totally fell apart. My advice? Think twice before sending your kids there to study! Below is a testimony from a young woman who was a student at Bill Johnson's Ministry School several years ago:

JOHANNA wrote:

In August 2008 I moved to Redding, California to attend Bethel School of Supernatural Ministry (BSSM). I graduated in May 2009... I went in expecting training for a life of ministry. Almost right away I began to question the bizarre behavior that is so normal there.

At Bethel, there are many sayings that are tossed around daily... "God only has nice things to say," "There's no high like the Most High." There would be all kinds of distracting behavior (random shouting, laughing, etc.) during school sessions and church services. When any guest speaker came to school, students would flock to the front to get as close to the speaker as possible. We were taught that any anointing we wanted could be received by simply "claiming it" for ourselves. Students would rush the stage and the front of the sanctuary so the speakers could lay hands on them.

Among the guest speakers were Bob Jones, Heidi Baker, Georgian and Winnie Banov, Randy Clark, John and Carol Arnott... Che Ahn, and Randall Worley. We also had regular sessions with Bill Johnson, Beni Johnson... and other Bethel pastors. The drunken behavior and questionable teachings from some, if not all, of these speakers was shocking at times. I can safely say that I never heard the word "repentance" once in any teaching.

I remember when the Banovs came, the whole place was complete chaos. When they touched someone, that person would jerk violently or stumble around as if they were drunk. The Banovs minister to people in trash dumps around the world... What I remember them talking about was love, joy, bliss, and the new wine.

I remember one day a Bethel pastor led us in what they call "encounters." The lights in the sanctuary were dimmed, they turned on "soaking music," and the woman instructed us all to find a comfortable place. What happened next was basically this pastor leading 800 students in a trance. She began to give us instructions like, 'Close your eyes and picture yourself in your favorite place. Now Jesus is going to walk towards you. What does he say? Now he's going to give you something. What is he giving you?...'

Angels were often talked about. I remember Beni Johnson actually took an RV across Arizona and New Mexico to wake up angels that were supposedly sleeping. (Another one of the common phrases, "Wakey wakey"). I would always hear people talking about their encounters with angels and how they visited heaven. One young woman I knew said she could see angels everywhere, she talked to them all the time, and she would help her friends to do the same.

Bethel is like Disneyland. It's dangerously easy to forget about everything else and instead focus on all there is to see and experience... God becomes like Santa Claus. Without the preaching of the true gospel, the fear of the Lord is lost.

Like Bill Johnson, Che Ahn is another pastor from California with a huge following and great respect in the Charismatic scene. But again, he was on stage to endorse and commission Todd Bentley at Lakeland - and there is no question that he is a "carrier" of this self-same anointing that we have been talking about. As someone wrote to me not long ago who had attended one of his meetings:

LUCY wrote:

In late October, after having attended the Fredericksburg (Virginia) Prayer Furnace at which Che Ahn ministered. There, I saw many of the manifestations you mention: hopping and jumping during "worship", falling backward at Che Ahn's touch, extreme jerkiness in several cases. Very uncomfortable with this, I came home and watched (my first time ever) videos of Todd Bentley. Needless to say, I was appalled...

THE TRUTH ABOUT "IHOP"

It gives me no pleasure, but rather a lot of grief and sadness to write about many of these things. In 1999 Mike Bickle, who had been pastor of the Kansas City Prophets' church (KC Metro), resigned from that position to start the 'House of Prayer' that had been on his heart for some time. But please remember, Bickle had personally defended the Toronto spirit and the "manifestations." He'd also invited John Arnott to speak in KC, and had led his church out of the Vineyard movement in protest when they expelled the main 'Toronto Blessing' church. So did any of this weird stuff seemingly follow him into his new House of Prayer (IHOP) movement? Yes, sadly it seems it did.

One of the major teachings that IHOP in Kansas City became known for is called the 'Bridal Paradigm'- Mike Bickle's specialist subject. Basically it takes the Song of Solomon and the concept of the 'Bride of Christ' to quite an extreme – where we are supposed to approach Jesus like a captivated lover – His "girlfriend" in a sense. In other words, even males are supposed to act towards God as though they are basically His lovesick "Brides". Personally I find it a very "sensual" approach to God – and I cannot find biblical backing for it at all. Below are several emails I received from readers, commenting on what they had seen or experienced regarding this teaching:

"R---" wrote:

I moved here to KC 2 years ago to attend IHOP.... I have been so confused by the whole up-sweep of the "Bridal Paradigm" and ravished heart of Jesus and Song of Solomon. I cannot relate to Jesus as romantic lover, nor do I want to!! I am trying to have clean thoughts and a pure heart. I want a Godly husband to be that for me, to model Christ's love and headship. All my friends tell me, "Jesus is your husband - let Him be your first love and your provider". As if I should shun men and give up on the idea of marriage.

"C---" wrote:

What's amazing is how the presence of this teaching is like yeast. For a few years I was among believers who had absorbed 'bridal paradigm' teaching out of KC. It had a weird way of rubbing off. Even though I'd never even encountered it myself directly, for awhile I'd unwittingly absorbed some of it & had some dreams I now know came from unclean spirits. Thankfully my discernment antennaes began picking up on & rejecting the unholy nature of all this. Like many such excesses, it's the mixture that results when deception is mingled with the pure revelation of the Spirit that's so very, very deadly.

From a BOOK that has been Required Reading at this IHOP School of Ministry in Kansas City:

"O Gaze Eternal,
How penetrating are Your Fires
Rushing through my darkest places
With the burning streams of Desire
Leaving me naked, purged and bare
... Yet embraced...
You take hold of my weakest places
And kiss them with Your mercy
Lifting up my low grounds
With your mighty love so holy..." (Pg 52).

"She lifted her arms wide to the Lord and said with all of her strength and her love, 'Enjoy me. Right here, right now, in my absolute weakness, enjoy me.'" (Pg 84).

The above book, which is entitled, "Deep Unto Deep – The Journey of the Embrace", goes on and on in a similar vein for 200 pages. We remind you again that this is an officially recommended publication at IHOP Kansas City, with a foreword by Mike Bickle himself. It has been "Required Reading" for the young people at their Ministry School.

(There are a number of books by IHOP founder Mike Bickle on this topic as well – such as "Passion For Jesus" and 'The Pleasures of Loving God'. I find them pretty distasteful, but not nearly as bad as the book quoted above).

When you hear people using such terms as the "ravished" heart of God, lovesick or 'swooning' for Jesus, inflamed or 'fascinated', etc, then you know that you are around people who are influenced by this teaching. Now, imagine the effect on both males and females when they are told to act like a lovesick, romantic 'bride' towards Jesus! I'm sure you can see how unclean spirits might quickly begin to take advantage of such a thing. And frankly, that is exactly what I believe has been happening in a number of cases. False sensual spirits have been getting involved.

In late 2009, IHOP in Kansas City began nightly meetings due to a 'revival' that they claimed had broken out there. So was it truly a pure move of God, or was it basically full of the same old "River"/ Toronto manifestations as elsewhere? Well, as two ex-IHOP people wrote to me:

SARAH wrote:

"I'm just about in tears over all of this...

I watched the very first nights of the recent "outpouring of the Holy Spirit" on the IHOP webstream and boy, did that turn sour fast. Aside from the singing on the first night, everything was just messed up. AHH! It's breaking my heart! How many people do we know and love in KC?!

I've watched my beloved siblings laugh uncontrollably, jerk as though sick, stumble and speak as though drunk, and "sing in tongues" in complete chaos and without interpretation. I've raised the issue among friends of being "drunk in the Spirit" and even though I prove over and over that God is for self-control, which they agree with, they continue to act like drunken fools! (See Titus 1:8 and 2:2; 1 Thessalonians 5:6-7 which compared in the NKJV and NIV relates self-control with being sober, pointing to the fact that the Holy Spirit is not one who takes delight in being drunk at

all, but in being sober-minded - fruit of the Spirit, what?)
Drunkenness is the complete opposite of being filled with the Holy
Spirit! For sober-mindedness is a filling of Him!; 1 Peter 1:13,
4:7, and 5:8..."

M---- wrote:

" *Now that IHOP is partnering with Toronto, Bill Johnson, and a*
bunch of the other guys who are big on signs and wonders and/ or
drunkenness in the spirit... If one of the fruits of the Holy Spirit is
self control, how can one say that the drunkenness and
manifestations are ˜from the same spirit? It does not make any
sense... Where in Scripture do we see Jesus having manifestations
or drunkenness? Its not in the Bible and it should not be in His
Church."

MIKE BICKLE'S DISTURBING DREAM

On February 13th, 2009, Mike Bickle had a very disturbing dream
which he published on the IHOP website because he felt it had
strong prophetic significance for the IHOP movement and others.
Below is the dream. See what you make of it:

MIKE BICKLE – Feb 13, 2009:

I had a long, vivid prophetic dream. I woke up at 2:30 AM with a
deep sense of reality.

In this dream I was in an outdoor conference with maybe 40,000
people. The conference venue was in an outdoor baseball stadium
in a large fair ground. I was preaching on prayer, power and end-
time judgment. I spoke at the two afternoon sessions. Leaders and
their people from many different charismatic streams were there. I
remember seeing Bill Johnson and his people at the conference.
We were enjoying warm fellowship together.

I finished preaching after the second session about 5 PM, when the
events of Rev. 12:7-9 began to occur. Demonic principalities were
being cast to the earth. They looked like very large snakes (over

100 yards long and 50 feet thick) with large heads that looked like a dragon. Many of them were descending from the sky down to the earth. No one at the conference had sufficient understanding or faith to respond in power and confidence. All the leaders and the people in the various charismatic streams ran in fear and confusion, including the IHOP people.

These snake-like-principalities were filled with rage against the people. These were angry and even humiliated about being confined to the earth.

The people were terrified. Along with the demons, soot or wet muddy thick ash also descended. It darkened the sky as it fell on the people. There was no home run fence at the end of the baseball field, so many of us were running from the stadium in that direction toward the park offices at the end of the large fair grounds.

All were running in fear and confusion. No one had good answers. I managed to get out of the vast fair grounds to the park offices (at the entrance). Wet ash was all over me as I ran. A lot of people didn't get out but were bitten by the snakes and covered with wet ash.

There were evil policeman at the entrance. They told me, "You have to go back into the fair grounds. You either go back in or we take you to prison." They were calloused about the danger I would face by going back into the fair grounds. I assumed they were in the Antichrist system. I was in a dilemma, I thought, "I just escaped from the most intense danger imaginable and I have to go back in". When standing by the police I thought, "I wish we would all have taken the End Times events more seriously back when we had time to prepare."

I said to myself, "the debate about power is much bigger than the power we actually walk in". I woke up with a sense of urgency... The point of the dream was to avoid the dilemma of being unprepared in that day... All of the different charismatic streams today (including IHOP) have empty arguments about power in the End Times drama without actually being prepared for that day..."

THE AUTHOR AGAIN: I just have a few simple questions about the above dream at this point. If the 40,000 in the stadium represent the number of people under the influence of the IHOP movement, then why did they have no defense against the "snake-demons" that came down and began to bite them? Why were the teachings of the leadership doing nothing to prepare them? Is it a coincidence that 'Kundalini' is always spoken of as a "serpent-type" spirit? And could it be that the "policemen" in the dream were actually God's servants preventing Mike Bickle from escaping the fate being suffered by his own people? A disturbing dream, indeed.

Strangely enough, having said all of this, I still have some regard for Mike Bickle and several of these other leaders whom we have mentioned. Not everything they say is "bad" – not by a long shot. But sadly I believe they are suffering under a spiritual delusion that is very serious – and I believe it is greatly affecting the people they are leading. The Kundalini spirit is a very serious deception, and we cannot afford to deal "lightly" with it in any sense. Thus I have to sadly issue the warning – "Stay away from IHOP"!

HEIDI& ROLLAND BAKER

A lot of people get quite upset when I include Rolland and Heidi Baker (from IRIS Ministries) on my Kundalini watch-list. They point out that they are doing wonderful work among the poor in Mozambique. Yes – I know! And I am all for the loving work that they are doing amongst the needy and the orphans. In fact, I am all for any message that they bring challenging the church to get involved in that kind of ministry. I believe strongly in ministering to the poor myself, and preach often on that topic. But none of that is the reason why I warn people against IRIS Ministries.

The fact is, these guys have been deeply into the whole "River"/ Manifestations movement for years. Heidi Baker is absolutely renowned for her weird Kundalini-like gyrations and "Wooahs" on stage. Not as bad as Stacey Campbell – but still pretty bad. And they have "imparted" this spirit to a lot of people as well. IRIS has it's main office in Redding connected with Bill Johnson. That entire circle is sadly infected with the same strange contagion. I wish it were not so – but it is, and we are forced to expose it to the light, lest the Body of Christ be even further damaged. I have nothing "personal" against any of these people. In fact, quite the reverse. But I simply believe we cannot allow this spirit to destroy any more of Christ's precious sheep.

LEAVING THE PROPHETIC MOVEMENT

Let me just return to my own personal journey for a few moments. By 2003, our ministry both internationally and in New Zealand had expanded by leaps and bounds. We were still "small," but over and over we had seen God multiplying the impact of the things we sent out. I had been involved in the Prophetic movement (mainly in 'Publishing') for ten years by this time. We had a book in the NZ Christian bookstores entitled, "The Coming Street Revival," and I was touring the nation preaching. Our international Email List had reached 5000 subscribers worldwide. But I was growing more and more unhappy with the Prophetic movement as time went on.

In 2003 God opened the door for me to minister across the USA – and He sent me there with an urgent warning for the church – that there was a limited "window" of time for that nation to come into true Revival – and what disasters would follow if she did not. It was a very sober, piercing word – a call to repentance and agonizing prayer.

After another lengthy ministry tour of the States that same year, God opened the door for our whole family to come and live in the USA. We settled in Kansas City – close to where the "action" was

– in early 2004. But it was to be a very tumultuous 2 ½ years there indeed.

The thing that finally pushed me out of the Prophetic movement altogether was a huge Conference that was held in the old 'Kansas City Prophets' building in late October 2004. The Conference was supposed to be the "return" of the Kansas City prophets – back to minister (at least on this one occasion) in KC again after all these years. The speakers were virtually a "Who's Who" of the biggest names in the movement – Bob Jones, John Paul Jackson, Bobby Conner, Paul Keith Davis – plus James Goll and more.

I have gone into more detail in other books about what happened during that Conference, so I don't want to repeat myself here. Suffice it to say that it finally confirmed to me beyond all doubt that the 'Prophetic' as it stood was basically beyond reforming – too far gone for words. As I wrote later:

"Virtually every day I came home utterly grieved and depressed. I had come to this conference with great expectancy and hope, thinking that the return of [the main prophet] may bring a renewal of all that was originally good about this movement. I literally came as a 'friend' and they turned me into an enemy in the space of three days..."

The very next day – October 31 st – Reformation Day – we were booked into the same auditorium for our own meeting. It basically turned out to be the day I announced my departure. But it wasn't until I sent the news out by email that the 'firestorm' began.

The email announcing my departure was entitled, "I'm Leaving the Prophetic Movement." It was published that same week. And what a commotion followed! I was literally inundated with thousands of responses from all over the world. I couldn't even read them all – there were so many. But as I said earlier, most seemed surprisingly supportive of the stand I'd taken.

I had always felt that my whole reason for coming to KC in the first place was to urge the movement back to it's original calling and mandate. Now I realized that this was not possible, and I knew

God wanted me out. In fact, I could see that this movement was now on such treacherous ground, and so deeply mired in deception, that it was literally becoming dangerous to partake of it in any way. Little did I know how much worse things were going to get in the years that followed.

CHAPTER FIVE

THE LAKELAND DISASTER

In March 2008, after four bruising years, my family and I departed the USA for a year's break in our home country of New Zealand – feeling quite discouraged and beaten down by the experiences we had gone through. Just a few weeks after our departure, a new movement began in the USA that was to have far-reaching consequences right around the world.

Of course, I knew Todd Bentley's ministry pretty well. In fact I had regarded him for some time as one of the "Top Three" most spiritually dangerous ministers in the Prophetic movement. So when news began to filter out that Todd was leading a new 'Healing revival' in Lakeland, Florida, I was quick to check it out. And I was not surprised at all to find it full of the same deceptive weirdness as before. In fact, if anything it seemed worse. And yet – *quelle surprise* – Charisma magazine already seemed to be trumpeting its praises. (But that was about to change in a big way – as we shall see).

The first email I sent out on our REVIVAL List about this new movement was dated April 23, 2008 – and it was entitled, "A False Healing Revival?? –Florida." Here is how it began:

Many of you will have already heard about the "Healing Revival" that has purportedly broken out in Lakeland, Florida. Today Charisma Magazine put out a piece on it entitled 'A Holy Ghost Outbreak in Florida' - "...Charismatics are flocking to the sleepy town of Lakeland, Fla. to attend evangelist Todd Bentley's unconventional revival services." Is Charisma preparing to hype this one to the skies like they did with Toronto and Rodney Howard-Browne? It seems perhaps they are.

But why am I opposed to this 'Healing Revival' so soon after it has been announced? -It is because I already know Todd Bentley's ministry all too well, and this whole thing centers around him.

Todd Bentley actually has deep roots in the Prophetic movement, and he is one of the very few ministers that I have ever felt I had to publicly warn people about by name. -His ministry is that bad. False "angel" encounters of the weirdest kind, gold dust, guided visualizations of the "Third Heaven" that are straight out of the New Age, etc. And yet there is a "power" with it that makes it all the more dangerous...

Yet seemingly, Charisma magazine was already treating Lakeland as the Next Big Thing: *"Many charismatics are wondering if the protracted meetings will become a phenomenon similar to what happened in Rodney Howard-Browne's meetings in Lakeland in 1993, at the Toronto Airport Vineyard Church in Canada in 1994 and at Brownsville Assembly of God in Pensacola in 1995..."*

But I reminded my readers of the warning from Lynn Clark, one of our main Moderators at 'RevivalSchool.com,' who had written:

"I bought Todd Bentley's teaching on third heaven visitations and brought it home to listen to. I was in my living room laying on the floor listening to the teaching on how to visualize the third heaven and what to say and was getting caught up into his teaching and all of a sudden I began to shake uncontrollably and jerk and groan, and no sooner had this taken place I became frozen stiff - I could not move any part of my body and I knew this was a demon trying to take hold of me, and so with all the effort I could muster I cried out, "God save me - Jesus help me" - and as soon as I cried out to the Lord my body went limp. God spared me that night and I will be forever grateful... I spent much of the night in tears asking God to forgive me - and renouncing all the hands layed on me and all the awful deception I had opened myself up to..."

After quoting Lynn's testimony in that first email, I went on to challenge Charisma magazine to thoroughly check out Todd's ministry before they put their full weight behind it:

I myself have heard the tapes of Todd Bentley's "Third Heaven Visualization" teachings, and I want to tell you - they are straight out of the New Age handbook. -Terrible stuff. And yet so widely accepted by thousands of Christians today.

Do these kinds of practices (above) produce a genuine 'Healing Revival'? -These are the kinds of questions that we need to be asking Charisma Magazine. I leave it for you to decide.

Of course, this first email caused an enormous wave of reaction – both for and against – right across the world. And no doubt a lot of readers were forwarding it to Charisma as well.

My next article came out a week later. It was entitled, "Angels & the Florida Healing Revival." Since I was getting so much flak from my first article, I knew I needed to explain why I felt it so necessary to sound the alarm:

Personally I am deeply saddened that I even have to put out these warnings. I get no pleasure out of it. In fact I hate having to talk about this stuff. But what happens if something is seriously amiss and yet no warnings are given? Is it right to be silent in such a case? What about the precious sheep? Shouldn't they be warned?

What a lot of people may not realize is that the leader of the revival Todd Bentley has a long history in the "Laughing/ Drunkenness" movement - but also is a leading proponent of strange "Angel" encounters (and I do mean 'strange'). Todd has openly promoted these encounters for years - in fact he is well-known for leading others into contact with these 'angels' too. This has been a big part of his ministry for a very long time. And it is really no different now.

I then went on to quote a couple of extracts from Todd's 2003 article 'Angelic Hosts':

"Father, give me the angels in heaven right now that are assigned to get me money and wealth. And let those angels be released on my behalf. Let them go into the four corners of the earth and gather me money"...

[Todd continued...]

"EMMA, ANGEL Of The PROPHETIC
Now let me talk about an angelic experience with Emma. Twice
Bob Jones asked me about this angel that was in Kansas City in
1980: "Todd, have you ever seen the angel by the name of Emma?"
He asked me as if he expected that this angel was appearing to me.
Surprised, I said, "Bob, who is Emma?" He told me that Emma
was the angel that helped birth and start the whole prophetic
movement in Kansas City in the 1980s. She was a mothering-type
angel that helped nurture the prophetic as it broke out. Within a
few weeks of Bob asking me about Emma, I was in a service in
Beulah, North Dakota.

"In the middle of the service I was in conversation with Ivan and
another person when in walks Emma. As I stared at the angel with
open eyes, the Lord said, "Here's Emma." I'm not kidding. She
floated a couple of inches off the floor. It was almost like Kathryn
Khulman in those old videos when she wore a white dress and
looked like she was gliding across the platform. Emma appeared
beautiful and young - about 22 years old - but she was old at the
same time. She seemed to carry the wisdom, virtue and grace of
Proverbs 31 on her life. She glided into the room, emitting brilliant
light and colors. Emma carried these bags and began pulling gold
out of them. Then, as she walked up and down the aisles of the
church, she began putting gold dust on people...

"Within three weeks of that visitation, the church had given me the
biggest offering I had ever received to that point in my ministry.
Thousands of dollars! Thousands!... During this visitation the
pastor's wife (it was an AOG church) got totally whacked by the
Holy Ghost - she began running around barking like a dog or
squawking like a chicken as a powerful prophetic spirit came on
her. Also, as this prophetic anointing came on her, she started
getting phone numbers of complete strangers and calling them up
on the telephone and prophesying over them... Then angels started
showing up in the church." [-'Angelic Hosts' by Todd Bentley].

I then added the following note: *"Lest anyone think that Todd may have changed his ways in recent times, you should know that he is constantly mentioning his 'angels' in the current Florida meetings also."*

THE "IMPARTATIONS" SPREAD...

Meanwhile the Lakeland revival was being broadcast around the world every night on God TV and the meetings were moved into an 8000-seater tent. The thing was exploding! And Todd was imparting his "anointing" to everyone he could – especially the leaders. An English preacher began what was called the "Dudley Outpouring" by bringing Todd's anointing back from Florida to the UK. Here were the manifestations that were being reported: *"Fire, a burning sensation, was felt all over people's bodies... There were outbursts of joy, drunkenness and spontaneous healings throughout the meeting."*

Other reports from the USA spoke of many pastors having hands laid on them to receive the "Florida anointing". Todd Bentley himself declared that this particular anointing was the most "contagious" that he had ever imparted to people. In a CBN News interview, he stated: *"Our focus here in Florida every night is I lay hands on every single person who comes - whether it's 5,000, 10,000 - And I'm praying every night, 'God, give it away, give it away, give it away.' And that's the focus here: Impartation."*

And indeed there were more and more reports of this anointing being transmitted from Florida to other states and nations across the globe. Prominent Charismatic leaders began to declare that this would be one of the greatest revival movements in history – maybe even the beginning of a "new awakening". The Elijah List proclaimed that on New Year's Eve, for 2008, God told Bob Jones that "the third wave was coming." Todd asked Bob what the third wave was. He said that, "Toronto was wave #1, Pensacola was wave #2, and the third wave is the "Winds of Change" -- this move of God. This move will be a global move, traveling with signs and wonders all over the world! The third wave is here!"

Meanwhile, there was I, seeming like the biggest fool on earth, standing right in the path of this juggernaut as it bore down on me like a runaway train. Only an idiot would stand in the way of such an acclaimed and magnificent movement – so it was thought. But suddenly Charisma began to ask questions as well, and the ballgame changed overnight. Not a lot. Not completely. But it did change. And suddenly the "juggernaut" began to look a little less invincible. This was the beginning of the most remarkable turn-around in the history of the "invasion". And before four months were out, events would occur that would stand the entire Charismatic world on it's head. But all that was yet to come...

LEE GRADY DARES TO QUESTION

On May 14th 2008 came the first of the Charisma questionings about Lakeland – by their Editor J. Lee Grady. I thought it was a very brave thing to do – because the entire Charismatic world was caught up in virtual "Lakeland-mania" by this time. Grady titled his article, "Honest Questions About the Lakeland Revival." Here were his opening remarks: *"I support any holy outbreak of revival fervor. But let's be careful to guard ourselves from pride and error."*

Grady spent much of the article seemingly trying to walk a "middle line" – but when he finally got to his "three warnings" for the Body of Christ, he pulled no punches. Here they are below:

1. Beware of strange fire...

I fear another message is also being preached subtly in Lakeland— a message that cult-watchers would describe as a spiritual counterfeit. Bentley is one of several charismatic ministers who have emphasized angels in the last several years. He has taught about angels who bring financial breakthroughs or revelations, and he sometimes refers to an angel named Emma who supposedly played a role in initiating a prophetic movement in Kansas City in the 1980s. Bentley describes Emma as a woman in a flowing white dress who floats a few feet off the floor...

We need to tread carefully here! We have no business teaching God's people to commune with angels or to seek revelations from them. And if any revival movement—no matter how exciting or passionate—mixes the gospel of Jesus with this strange fire, the results could be devastating...

2. Beware of bizarre manifestations...

In many recent charismatic revivals, ministers have allowed people to behave like epileptics on stage—and they have attributed their attention-getting antics to the Holy Spirit. We may think it's all in fun (you know, we're just "acting crazy" for God) but we should be more concerned that such behavior feeds carnality and grieves the Spirit.

When exotic manifestations are encouraged, people can actually get a religious high from jerking, vibrating, screaming or acting intoxicated. (I have even been around people who writhed as if in pain, or made sexual noises—thinking this was a legitimate spiritual experience.)...

3. Beware of hype and exaggeration...

Some of the language used during the Lakeland Revival has created an almost sideshow atmosphere. People are invited to "Come and get some." Miracles are supposedly "popping like popcorn." Organizers tout it as the greatest revival in history...

I was deeply impressed with this article. Despite clearly still treating Lakeland as a "true revival," Lee Grady had managed to trumpet some real warnings to the Body of Christ. At least somebody was concerned for the precious sheep! And this was just the first of many alarms that Lee Grady would raise.

BIZARRE MANIFESTATIONS

Meanwhile however, the Lakeland 'anointing' was spreading unhindered around the globe. The meetings in Florida were growing mightily and hundreds upon hundreds of leaders were rushing there for an "impartation" and taking it back to their own people. One eyewitness described the impartation lines in Florida this way: *"As far (and I mean as far) as I could see, masses of people on the floor shaking, shivering, dazed looking, completely out or unconscious looking."*

A man from Clearwater, Florida wrote to me that a number of people from his fellowship had attended the revival and then brought the 'anointing' back with them. Here is what he described:

"These are the effects that I have witnessed on people who have attended this movement and either have had hands laid on them or claim to have been imparted with "the spirit":
-They come back with this kind of childlike drunken stupor.
-Descriptions of a burning sensation either in their veins, heads or stomachs.
-Dancing about like drunk...
-Inappropriate yelling and screaming like they're at a football game;
-Young men whistling over and over and holding their heads and claiming that they "feel the Holy Spirit about to split them in two"...
-Women just gyrating and pulsating like they're being ravaged from behind from some unseen force.
-Drunken uncontrollable laughter in the middle of a solemn prayer time
-People being "slain in the spirit"... just falling down and being unable to move (like something's holding them down)..."

Another eyewitness from Hawaii reported the arrival of the 'Florida anointing' there: *" As the Pastor laid hands on the people he yelled with great force, "FIRE!!!" Folks dropped like flies. People were all over the floor... howling, crying and sobbing in anguish, laughing, shaking, some convulsing under the power, and falling as if some thunder fell on their heads."*

Another man from the U.S. Northeast wrote:

I went to West Haven, CT, last weekend... Some of them had been to Lakeland and were jerking and yelling "Oh-woooooooowwww" and then they began to talk about how Bob Jones called it the 3rd wave... They all were in what they call Drunken Glory... They are having services all over for impartation and daily reports are breaking out about it. I am being told that I am deceived for questioning it. They are telling me that I am going against the Holy Spirit...

Months later another woman wrote to me of her own experience:

I went to Lakeland 3 times. I was so drawn to go there. I really thought it was of God... I had so many supernatural experiences – to seeing a mystical Jesus with a third eye, angels talking to me, visions, being transported. I had one experience with my daughter being in the room and her experiencing it too. I was roaring like a lion, had gold dust and many other experiences. The worst thing that happened to me is that it got sexual. This false Jesus was approaching me sexually and I fell into it. I still to this day do not understand how I could have been so deceived. I have been a Christian since the age of 16. I am 49 now... I fell right in... hook, line and sinker. When I came home that last visit I became aware it was demonic, and I was surrounded and covered with demons literally, it was so horrible, all that I went through, you cannot imagine... I was seeing demons and being touched sexually and tormentingly constantly.. it has been 1 1/2 years and I am still battling these demonic spirits. I cry out to the Lord everyday for total deliverance. It has been horrible. I have renounced and repented, but still fighting. How do we get free of this?

Another woman also wrote to me later – and you can see how even good Christians could be caught up in this movement:

When the revival in Lakeland first started... You issued a warning on that list and I defended Todd. My motive was not to be

71

judgmental toward him. I, like others, have been so hungry for God to do something in this terrible situation we find ourselves in this country. I was wrong. Wrong to defend Todd and wrong to attack you. All I can do is say I do see the light. This happened one night when I saw a woman, which I clearly saw under the influence of a demonic spirit brought up on the platform and encouraged. She was going through such contortions that the was literally at times standing on her neck with her body absolutely straight up in the air. The poor woman must have suffered terribly from the rug burns she experienced that night...

When I first came into the charismatic movement in the mid 70's it was a wonderful experience--very Biblical and, you're right, the manifestations we saw with Todd were considered demonic at that time and people were ministered to for deliverance...

CHARISMA QUESTIONS AGAIN

On May 28th, Lee Grady waded into the Lakeland controversy once more with another incisive article. He called it, "An Appeal for Unity in a Divisive Season".

Near the start he made quite an interesting point about the 'messiness' of Revivals: *"Revival is messy. As much as we would love for it to come in a neat and orderly package, history teaches us that outbreaks of the Holy Spirit are often accompanied by holy chaos. There may be conversions and healings in one corner and demonic manifestations in the other. In seasons of revival you can have miracles and mayhem. Holiness and heresy can erupt simultaneously..."*

My own reply at the time was that – *"Yes - Revivals are often messy - but they are messy around the FRINGES - not at the very heart and center of what is happening. As many readers know, I have been studying Revival history for many years and I have a whole chapter on "Manifestations in Revivals" in my new book... But the fact is, if you have demonic deception right at the center of what is being preached or imparted, then you no longer just have a "messy" revival - you have a deadly counterfeit. True Revivals always have pure preaching of Repentance, Holiness and the Cross at the center...*

We are not dealing with a movement that has problems around the "fringes" here. The problems are right at the heart - ie. they involve the central things that are being preached and imparted to people from the front. And it has been that way from the start – which is what makes this crucially different from a real Revival. I hope, Lee, that you can see what an important distinction this is?"

The Charisma editor again seemed to spend most of his new article treading a "middle path." But again, when he did deliver some punches near the end, he didn't hold back:

"... leaders must address all of the difficult issues triggered by the Lakeland Revival. Those include:

1. Biblical guidelines about angels. Some people in the prophetic camp speak of frequent visits to heaven, 'third heaven revelations,' and long conversations with angels who use names such as Emma, Promise and Winds of Change. Are these indeed spirits sent from God, or agents of false light?

2. A proper theology of the dead. Some in the prophetic camp claim they have had conversations with dead Christians – including Paul the apostle. Is this within the bounds of Christian experience, or is it necromancy?

3. Pastoral guidance about exotic spiritual manifestations. In some circles in our movement, unusual signs and wonders have been reported in church services - including the sudden appearance of gold dust, feathers, gemstones and oil. At the same time, worshipers are vibrating on the floor, jerking uncontrollably and acting intoxicated. How can we protect people from the abuse of manifestations, and from demonic influence, while at the same time leaving room for genuine encounters with God?

4. Clear guidelines concerning the restoration of fallen ministers. The appearance of one prominent fallen evangelist, Paul Cain, at the Lakeland Revival in May unleashed strong reactions from many sectors of the church..."

Again, some bold and incisive questioning from Lee Grady – trying to protect the precious sheep. At the time, Lee was virtually the only prominent leader in the Charismatic world that was willing to put himself on the line over these issues. And this would not be the last time, either. Over coming months the Charisma editor would again take on the Lakeland juggernaut with articles such as, "Bam! Pow! When Prayer Ministry Gets Violent" (aimed at the antics of Todd Bentley when he prayed for people) and "The Marks of Genuine Revival – Part One and Two."

But Lakeland was a long way from being finished yet. It was still a rampaging train, with the backing of the vast majority of the Charismatic world. All we could do was warn those who would listen. But after June 23rd, 2008, that became even harder. For that was the day when all the famous leaders "commissioned" Todd Bentley live on television. Little did we know, however, that this would be the beginning of the end.

THE GREAT "COMMISSIONING"

Here is how Charisma announced the news of what took place in Lakeland that fateful day of June 23rd: *"Leaders Commission Todd Bentley at 'Lakeland Outpouring'... The special service was billed by leaders as one of the greatest moments in revival history."*

The article continued:

"Participating leaders at the ceremony included [C. Peter] Wagner; Ché Ahn, pastor of Harvest Rock Church in Pasadena, Calif.; John Arnott of Toronto Airport Christian Fellowship in Canada; Bill Johnson, pastor of Bethel Church in Redding, Calif.; and Rick Joyner, founder of MorningStar Ministries in Charlotte, N.C."

Other notables also lent their support from afar. As Peter Wagner wrote shortly afterward: *"Unfortunately Bishop Bill Hamon had to cancel because of a travel problem"* and *"Che, Bill and John laid on hands and anointed Todd with a special new "Be Revived" oil that Chuck Pierce (who was in Africa) sent for the event."*

Wagner, recognized by many as the "leading apostle" of the Charismatic world, led the ceremony – calling it an "apostolic alignment." He made the following statement before all the TV cameras and all the people:

"I take the apostolic authority that God has given me and I decree to Todd Bentley:

-Your power will increase.

-Your authority will increase.

-Your favor will increase.

-Your influence will increase.

-Your revelation will increase.

I also decree that:

-A new supernatural strength will flow through this ministry.

-A new life force will penetrate this move of God..."

Wagner later called this a "groundbreaking event" and stated that, "We are now in a place in what I see as the Second Apostolic Age..." (In other words, a 'new era' of real apostles).

Those who saw the video of this commissioning may also have noticed that Stacey Campbell, one of the main 'Toronto' leaders who spoke, had her head shaking so violently – literally whipping back and forth – that it was hard to hear her. Of course this happened all the time and they claimed it was the "Holy Spirit".

Todd Bentley later said: *"I am no church historian, but I do not know of any other time in history, since the book of Acts, have so many different apostles and so many different prophets and movements and leaders [been represented]."*

I must say, I didn't find Todd Bentley's comment to be particularly "humble" – especially given later events. However, for me, one of the most grievous statements of all came towards the end of the Charisma article:

"Leaders who have expressed private concerns about Bentley's ministry turned down Charisma's request for public comment."

Here is the statement I made concerning this "lack of public comment" at the time:

Did you see that last sentence? -Even though some leaders have been privately expressing their concerns, they actually refused an opportunity to speak out in public! So where does this leave the poor sheep? Are these men so concerned with their "reputation" that they are afraid to speak out at such a pivotal moment? How will history judge such a thing? Isn't it simply the "fear of man"? And isn't this the exact reason why the Charismatic movement is in such a mess in the first place? Have we completely forgotten the old saying- "Evil prospers when good men do nothing"?

Privately, however, despite this "fighting talk," I was personally devastated by the events of June 23. It was true that our warnings were being widely distributed, but I had never felt so lonely. Now, it seemed, the "biggest guns" of the Charismatic world were standing openly against us. I was deeply discouraged.

By this time we had a book out on Amazon about Lakeland called "True & False Revival," and I was literally doing everything I could to warn the Body of Christ. But it all seemed in vain. Every week things seemed to grow worse and worse. The contagion was now planet-wide – and spreading faster than ever.

But God was far from discouraged. Things were about to change in a massive way. In fact – for reasons we will discuss later – I am convinced that God deliberately waited until after this "commissioning" before He started to unravel this highly-touted spectacle that was the Lakeland revival. And when the unraveling began, it was literally amazing how quickly things came apart. God will not be mocked.

THE INFAMOUS TV INTERVIEW

On July 9, 2008, ABC Nightline aired a TV special on the Lakeland revival. Though they called Lakeland an "international sensation" and showed many people coming from all over the world, the piece was certainly not favorable to Todd Bentley. The most shocking thing to Christians was that when Nightline asked for "just three" medically verifiable healings, they were given very patchy or unsubstantiated information. In the end they made the statement, "Not a single miracle claim of Bentley's could be verified." This was an especially jarring statement to fans of the revival. The piece also featured Christians who questioned the circus-like atmosphere and the "BAMS" yelled by Todd Bentley as he prayed for people.

Overnight there was an enormous change. Bentley left the revival for a number of days – only returning on July 18. But things were never the same. Was it really true that there were so few verifiable healings? What about all the claims of "raisings from the dead," etc?

On July 14 and 16, one of Peter Wagner's own "apostles" broke his silence and spoke out publicly for the first time. Robert Ricciardelli was a "marketplace apostle" in Peter Wagner's 'International Coalition of Apostles' (ICA) as well as being a Charisma Magazine writer and a friend of Lee Grady.

On July 16th he commented on one Internet blog:

"Truth is there are very few people being healed in Lakeland. I have worked with Charisma Magazine editor Lee Grady in discovering how many false reports have been released as facts." Concerning the 'Resurrections' in Lakeland, Robert wrote on another blog: *"We have investigated the 20 plus "raised from the dead" claims as we want to report them to the media, and they cannot be verified..."*

On our own Forum at RevivalSchool.com, Robert publicly added the following statements:

77

"... we may not be a part of the ICA if Peter and the leadership do not reconsider their impromptu decision to jump into the Lakeland stream, when many of us warned him not to... The biggest thing about Lakeland is the lack of the fear of our Awesome God, lack of repentance and humility. Many have exchanged the truth for a lie and chosen experience over content. Angels, trances, and 3rd heaven focus has replaced the gospel as a focus."

He went on to say:

" The transferring of anointing, the focus on man bringing anything but the gospel is amazing and sad... if Peter Wagner, Bill Johnson, and some distinguished members of the Who's Who in Charismania say it is all good, then people just go with it. Some have begun to see the YouTube and other information and begun to change. Some go as far as to claim it as deception, others say it is a move of God that needs correction... It is my opinion that it was man orchestrated and demonically influenced from the very beginning.

Bentley is just a product of the Charismatic/ apostolic/ prophetic trending away from Plumb line truth...I wrote an article for Charisma that everything that can be shaken is being shaken, and this is what is happening in a great way right now..."

THE DISASTER GETS WORSE

It was very soon after this that Bentley announced he would be leaving the revival permanently after August 23rd. But then he dropped another bombshell: He and his wife were separating. And it turned out that there was "another woman" involved – one of his female staff members at the revival that he had developed a "relationship" with. The whole nightmare then began to take on a very unearthly feel. And the big leaders who had stood on that stage commissioning and prophesying over Bentley just weeks earlier seemed to hardly know what to do with themselves – they were so embarrassed.

The breakup of Todd's marriage sent a massive shockwave through the entire Charismatic movement worldwide. Many were deeply shaken. Lee Grady spoke for a lot of Charismatics when he wrote: *"I'm sad. I'm disappointed. And I'm angry."* His article was called, "Life After Lakeland: Sorting Out the Confusion." Here are some extracts:

Todd Bentley's announcement that his marriage is ending has thrown our movement into a tailspin—and questions need to be answered …

From the first week of the Lakeland revival, many discerning Christians raised questions about Bentley's beliefs and practices. They felt uneasy when he said he talked to an angel in his hotel room. They sensed something amiss when he wore a T-shirt with a skeleton on it. They wondered why a man of God would cover himself with tattoos. They were horrified when they heard him describe how he tackled a man and knocked his tooth out during prayer...

Why did God TV tell people that "any criticism of Todd Bentley is demonic"?

This is cultic manipulation at its worst. The Bible tells us that the Bereans were noble believers because they studied the Scriptures daily "to see whether these things were so" (Acts 17:11, NASB)... We are commanded to test the spirits...

Why did a group of respected ministers lay hands on Bentley on June 23 and publicly ordain him? Did they know of his personal problems?...

I trust that Wagner, Ahn, Johnson and Arnott didn't know of Bentley's problems before they ordained him.... But I believe that they, along with Bentley and the owners of God TV, owe the body of Christ a forthright, public apology...

Sadly, there was no apology forthcoming – except from Dutch Sheets – who had not even been at the Commissioning himself. The rest mostly seemed content to try to "spin" their way out of the whole disaster or distance themselves from it in some way. There were very few "Sorries". And a lot of leaders around the world who had been right into Lakeland – and leading their people into it, suddenly just stopped talking about it altogether. Almost no apologies were ever issued. I guess a simple question at this point might be - "Can God really trust leaders like that to tend His precious sheep?"

Speaking personally, I was so stunned and shocked by this sudden turn of events that I hardly knew how to react. Some might think I would be delighted at this sudden vindication. After all, by this time I had been fighting a lonely rearguard action for 14 years against the whole thing – basically losing all the way. Perhaps, some might think, I was entitled to a bout of self-congratulation. But that is not the way it was. I simply felt empty. Vindicated – yes. But the ending of Todd's marriage was nothing to celebrate. The tragedy of a Christian marriage ending in such a fashion should bring grief, never joy. I guess I just felt stunned and sad on behalf of the entire church for the whole sorry mess.

There is no question though, that it bought about a huge over-turning of that spirit's stronghold in the church. And I don't believe it will ever fully recover. Too many people now questioned the whole thing.

Fourteen years of 'Kundalini' - fourteen years that the locusts had eaten. I thought maybe now it was over. But sadly I thought wrong.

RICK JOYNER'S ROLE

Personally I had always tried to go somewhat "easy" on Rick Joyner up until Lakeland. At the time that I left the Prophetic movement in late 2004, I had written:

A number of people asked me about Rick Joyner and Morningstar Ministries. Where do they fit into all this? Well, seemingly Rick has always managed to keep himself at a slight distance from the worst excesses and controversies of this movement. (-Except for when he joined the Knights of Malta - an ancient Catholic Order. -By the way, that is probably what led to the fad of using swords to 'knight' people that swept through this movement a few years ago). I have read some of Joyner's books and enjoy some of the things he says, but frankly, just because he has kept himself at a slight distance does not absolve him from the mess that the Prophetic is in today. The fact is, Mr Joyner is very close friends with almost all of the main leaders at this recent conference. He regularly ministers alongside them - and knows them very well. As a 'father' in the movement, if he had brought correction it would have been heeded, but he has clearly failed to do so. Thus, he has to be held accountable for the state of things as much as anyone else. And it would not surprise me if similar deception is finding it's way into Morningstar conferences. (-A number of the same people are involved). Sadly then, I have had to remove any articles or links to Rick Joyner from my web-site - along with all the others.

However, it was not until Rick Joyner publicly endorsed Lakeland that I became truly outspoken about his ministry.

JOYNER "RESCUES" TODD

On March 9, 2009, Rick Joyner announced that Todd Bentley was now divorced and re-married to the female staff member that he had become involved with during the revival. Rick Joyner also announced that Bentley had relocated to his (Joyner's) ministry in North Carolina where he would be involved in a process of "restoration" – aimed at returning him to active ministry once again. Lee Grady, for one, seemed incensed at the way this was being handled. In an article entitled, "The Tragic Scandal of Greasy Grace," he wrote:

In all the discussion of Bentley and the demise of the Lakeland Revival, I am waiting to hear the sound of sackcloth ripping into shreds. We should be weeping. We should be rending our hearts – as God commanded Israel when they fell into sin (see Joel 2: 13-14). To give guidance to a confused church, our leaders should have publicly decried the Lakeland disaster while at the same time helping both Todd and Shonnah to heal.

We have not mourned this travesty. We have not been shocked and appalled that such sin has been named among us. We act as if flippant divorce and remarriage are minor infractions - when in actuality they are such serious moral failures that they can bring disqualification...

THE BIG COMEBACK

Only ten months later in January 2010 came the announcement by Rick Joyner and Todd Bentley that he was back ministering on-stage at Joyner's large conference center. And there was live TV of it going out worldwide. Already they were hinting that this was the beginning of a "new revival."

Immediately I sent out an email notice to our readers, entitled "Kundalini Warning – Urgent." In it I wrote:

I just saw the video of Rick Joyner announcing that Todd Bentley is back ministering every night at Morningstar in North Carolina and now they have so-called "revival" manifestations eerily similar to Lakeland. They also announced that they are streaming these big meetings every night on their new TV channel - and they are greatly promoting the whole thing.

Rick Joyner has been warned very specifically by high-level ministries not to do what he is doing now - bringing Todd Bentley back into the limelight... Apparently the "manifestations" are all that matter... Do we not realize that many false religions have their own version of "laying on of hands" that results in these very types of manifestations?

When you see videos of these "kriyas" or other Kundalini-type manifestations, you would often swear that you are watching a modern "Impartation"-type church meeting. (And I say this as someone who believes strongly in the gifts of the Holy Spirit. I just don't believe in "alien" anointings infiltrating the Body of Christ! There is a big difference between Kundalini and the real Holy Spirit)...

This is a powerful spirit and it has the backing of a lot of big-name ministries. In fact, these men and women are the very ones responsible for allowing it to spread right through the body of Christ. And one day they will be answerable to God for doing so.

THE FATE OF TODD BENTLEY

For a time in 2010 Todd Bentley remained ministering regularly onstage at Morningstar in North Carolina, with live television feeds going out all over the world. He also began gathering "partners" and rebuilding his ministry base. Clearly this was his attempt at a comeback. But it would never truly take off. I guess even the Charismatic movement has its' limits of what it will tolerate. Ironically, the movement seemed fine with a lot of the jerking, the laughter, the vibrations, the strange 'angels,' the "drunken glory" and the outright heresy being transmitted at Lakeland. But when Todd split from his wife – that was the limit. They could accommodate a New Age invasion on a worldwide scale. But not a marriage breakup.

Todd Bentley's new wife Jessa clearly supports the extreme manifestations that her husband has come to represent. A popular Youtube video shows her 'prophesying' onstage with her head jerking side to side convulsively - very similar to Stacey Campbell. Her new husband Todd looks on approvingly.

In August 2012, Bentley was scheduled to minister at a series of meetings in England, Wales and Ireland. Surprisingly the UK government announced that they were banning him from entering the country. The UK's Home Office announced, *"The government makes no apologies for refusing people access to the UK if we believe they are not conducive to the public good. Coming here is a privilege that we refuse to extend to those who might seek to undermine our society."* Bentley was understandably said to be extrememly upset at the news.

In April 2013, Todd Bentley and his 'Fresh Fire USA' team began daily meetings at a place called Tongaat in South Africa. These meetings had a similar flavor to Lakeland, and before long there was a great deal of hype flowing about 'healings,' etc. God TV even announced that they would be regularly broadcasting what was taking place. After a few weeks the meetings were moved to the capital city Durban, where they slowly petered out. I guess even South Africa is not far enough away for Bentley to escape his tarnished past.

And so it goes on. Most likely, Todd Bentley will continue on this way for years – popping up in various parts of the world. But I do not believe he will ever be the force that he once was. The Kundalini invasion does not need Todd Bentley to keep on advancing. There is an entire army of preachers out there today who move in the same "anointing." And still it spreads. No Todd Bentley required.

A CHURCH IN NEED OF DELIVERANCE

When an individual person has been "invaded" by an unclean spirit, we say that that person needs 'deliverance' to drive it out. And usually the first step is Repentance. Well, the Body of Christ is in need of deliverance today. And I believe that great repentance is also required. We cannot play games with what I believe is a 'New Age'-type spirit that has invaded on a large scale. Kundalini is never something to take lightly. And it is still rampant in whole sections of the Body today. A massive "clean-out" is required.

Despite the shockwave that reverberated around the world with the collapse of Lakeland, most of the "players" in that circle did not seem to change greatly or repent of the 'spirit' that they had been operating under. It is still business as usual. That is why we need a another 'Great Reformation' in the Body of Christ. God simply cannot have leaders over His church in the last days that utterly lack discernment. He cannot have it. We need a changing of the guard. And I believe we need to see this spirit utterly "expelled" from the church. It does not belong – and should be given no place.

CHAPTER SIX

VISIONS OF WARNING

Over the years there have been many visions or prophecies seeking to warn the Body of Christ of exactly the type of deception that we have seen invade the church over the last 20 years. Below are several of the most significant and insightful ones that I have come across:

1965 VISION OF COMING DECEPTION

-by Stanley Frodsham.

Below is an excerpt from a prophecy given in 1965 by Stanley Frodsham – a Spirit-filled preacher and author of the well-known book, "Smith Wigglesworth: Apostle of Faith."

"...Do not hold men's persons in admiration. For many whom I shall anoint mightily, with signs and miracles, shall be lifted up and shall fall away by the wayside. I do not do this willingly; I have made provision that they might stand. I call many into this ministry and equip them; but remember that many shall fall. They shall be like bright lights and people shall delight in them. But they shall be taken over by deceiving spirits and shall lead many of My people away.

"Hearken diligently concerning these things, for in the last days will come seducing spirits that shall turn many of My anointed ones away. Many shall fall through various lusts and because of sin abounding. But if you will seek Me diligently, I will put My Spirit within you. When one shall turn to the right hand or to the left you shall not turn with them, but keep your eyes wholly on the Lord. The coming days are most dangerous, difficult and dark, but there shall be a mighty outpouring of My Spirit upon many cities.

My people must be diligently warned concerning the days that are ahead. Many shall turn after seducing spirits; many are already seducing My people. It is those who do righteousness that are righteous. Many cover their sins by theological words. But I warn you of seducing spirits who instruct My people in an evil way.

"Many shall come with seducing spirits and hold out lustful enticements. You will find that after I have visited My people again, the way shall become more and more narrow, and fewer shall walk therein. But be not deceived, the ways of righteousness are My ways. For though Satan comes as an angel of light, hearken not to him; for those who perform miracles and speak not righteousness are not of Me. I warn you with great intensity that I am going to judge My house and have a church without spot or wrinkle when I come. I desire to open your eyes and give you spiritual understanding, that you may not be deceived but may walk in uprightness of heart before Me, loving righteousness and hating every evil way. Look unto Me, and I will make you to perceive with eyes of the Spirit the things that lurk in darkness that are not visible to the human eye. Let me lead you in this way that you may perceive the powers of darkness and battle against them. It is not a battle against flesh and blood; for if you battle in that way, you accomplish nothing. But if you let Me take over and battle against the powers of darkness, than they are defeated, and then liberation is brought to My people.

"I warn you to search the Scriptures diligently concerning these last days. For the things that are written shall indeed be made manifest. There shall come deceivers among My people in increasing numbers who shall speak for the truth and shall gain the favor of the people. For the people shall examine the Scriptures and say, 'What these men say is true'. Then when they have gained the hearts of the people, then and only then shall Satan enter into My people. Watch for seducers.

"Be not deceived. For the deceiver will first work to gain the hearts of many, and then shall bring forth his insidious doctrines. You cannot discern those that are of Me and those that are not of Me

when they start to preach. But seek Me constantly, and then when these doctrines are brought out you shall have a witness in your heart that these are not of Me. Fear not, for I have warned you. Many will be deceived. But if you walk in holiness and uprightness before the Lord, your eyes shall be open and the Lord will protect you. If you will constantly look unto the Lord, you will know when the doctrine changes and will not be brought into it. If your heart is right I will keep you; and if you will constantly look to Me, I will uphold you.

"The minister of righteousness shall be on this wise: his life shall agree with the Word and his lips shall give forth that which is wholly true, and it will be no mixture. When the mixture appears, then you will know he is not a minister of righteousness. The deceivers speak first the truth then error, to cover their own sins which they love. Therefore, I exhort and command you to study the Scriptures relative to seducing spirits, for this is one of the great dangers of these last days.

"I desire you to firmly be established in My Word and not in the personalities of men that you will not be moved as so many shall be moved. Take heed to yourselves and follow not the seducing spirits that are already manifesting themselves. Diligently inquire of Me when you hear something that you have not seen in My Word, and do not hold people's persons in admiration--for it is by this very method Satan will destroy many of My people."

THE ACID CLOUD - A VISION (-Excerpts)

-by Richard Smith.

This vision emerged with an unusually vivid degree of clarity on Thursday morning the 29th September, 1994...

Following a period of pouring out my distressed feelings about the condition of the Church to Jesus, who is our heavenly Advocate, I saw ahead of me a large billowing black cloud which carried lots of soot and other pollutants. Its sulphurous stench revealed that here was no natural cloud, but rather it was the type of acid cloud which arises from the explosion of some chemical plant or oil installation. Blown by its own momentum, the acid cloud was rapidly heading towards a low waterless desert plain which lay beneath some rocky mountains. Filling the plain were all types of people whom I understood represented the Christian population of England. Most were indigenous white Anglo-Saxons, but there were members of various ethnic minorities as well. These stood for the immigrant population in England.

FOUR GROUPS. On closer inspection, I could see that this vast assembly was divided into four main groups. The first of these was the one that was nearest to the cloud and was obviously coming under its influence. This particular group can be known as the intoxicated. Behind them, closely intermingled together, were the second and third groups - these can be known as the fearful and the angry. Still further behind at a little distance was a smaller group who will be known as the prepared. However, one fact was obvious - the acid cloud was going to cover all four groups regardless of whether they wanted it to or not.

It was at this point that I perceived that the cloud was blowing in from the Westerly direction.

In response to this cloud, the first group were laughing, dancing and singing. A few of their members were lying prostrate and making all kinds of animal noises. Some were so deliriously happy that they actually formed a dance line, which - while they were dancing the conga - snaked its way into the cloud. With a start, I realised their mistake. Already intoxicated by invisible fumes emanating from the front of the cloud, this group were wrongly assuming that the polluted cloud was a refreshing rain cloud that represented God's presence. They failed to see what its true nature was...

1) The acid cloud not only represented what is currently known as the Toronto Phenomenon, it also represents all that will come out of that occurrence. The Toronto Phenomenon is so to speak only the front edge of the cloud. It is paving a way for even more

extreme manifestations of the evil one. In short, "Toronto" can be seen as a beginning rather than an end.

2) Being blown by its own momentum indicates that within the cloud there is only what can be described as a hostile alien spirit. It is the head spirit of many other spirits which inhabit the cloud. Moreover, this alien spirit has been given permission by God to try the loyalties of Christians in this country. Through a process of sharp division, which will cause many wounds, it will become really clear who in the Church is standing by Jesus and who is not. However, some of those who belong to the first three groups will be given a few further chances to repent. For a little while, the opportunity to get back into a right relationship with God will exist.

By no means will all Christians survive the passing of the cloud. Some will forsake their faith, while others will suffer from permanent physical and mental breakdowns. A few will even lose their very lives there.

I began to see that the acid cloud was also the cloud of God's judgement, that will have to pass over the Church until evil is forcibly removed from it. Only after the acid cloud has done its work will the Church be pure enough to receive the cloud of God's presence. This cloud will in turn bring further cleansing and much-needed revival. However, the time for this second cloud to pass over is not yet. Any hopes of immediate revival are therefore premature. This means that taken as a whole, the Toronto Phenomenon does not represent a time of refreshing, rather it represents what is perhaps the first installment of a VERY severe judgement on the churches in this country.

In a very real sense, the mass of God's people are being handed over to satan for the destruction of the flesh. Only those who are faithful to the Lord in all things will be exempt from this judgement – even though they may be distressed by its consequences.

JOEL'S ARMY & GIDEON'S ARMY – A VISION
-by Robert I. Holmes.
Excerpts from the founder of 'Storm-Harvest' in Australia.

In late October 1996 I had a startling vision. I was looking down from a high place and I saw a mighty army. It was marching in a long line, like a great column snaking through the jungle. It looked for all the world like a serpent. At it's head was a banner, which read "Joel's army". Behind them they left a swath of destruction, a road of sorts cut through the jungle. I was made aware that this army was 'now marching' or had already mobilised.

I also saw off to one side, hidden in dense undergrowth, a battalion. This group stood quietly, waiting in the jungle. They were assembled in a square, and they were awaiting instructions. At the head of this smaller group was a banner which read "Gideon's army".

JOEL'S ARMY

Joel's army has been promoted widely as being a good army, an army of the church. Many songs, sung in Pentecostal and mainline Evangelical churches even quote the warrior Scriptures as relating to the church. However I do not hold to that understanding. To me, Joel's army is one of terrible locusts, "a great and powerful army... before them is like Eden, after them is desolate" (Joel 2:2,3). This is similar to the picture I had. Joel says they are "a powerful army, drawn up for battle, before them the nations are in anguish" (5, 6). Why are the nations terrified of this army? Because they are an instrument of judgement.

Note that the Scripture does not say, "God's enemies are in anguish before them." Nor does it imply that the devil is afraid of them. It is the nations who are afraid. This army is made up of "the cutting locust... the swarming locust... the hopping locust... the destroying locust" (Joel 1:4). This is not a picture of the Bride of Christ. Evidently the army first destroys or brings judgement against God's own people because later in the book of Joel, God consoles His people saying, "I will repay YOU for the years the swarming locust has eaten, the hopper, the destroyer and the cutter, that great army I sent against you" (Joel 2:25).

This is clearly God's instrument of judgement against both his church and the nations (peoples), not a great or good army in the church! The passages relating to Joel's army confuse some, because it is said that the Lord is at the head of HIS army. He is in control of them. But that no more makes them the church than it made Babylon or Assyria the church! Jeremiah depicts Babylon as God's own instrument, his servant (Jer 25:9), just as Isaiah depicts Assyria as being a weapon in God's hand (Isa 7:20). God used them, as He uses the army depicted by Joel, to berate and scold an unrepentant Israel. In the same way, Joel's army is marching in the end times, to scold and rebuke, to consume and devour the unregenerate church.

I was impressed that this army was "now marching". There is only one globally significant move underfoot at this time. It has already affected many churches, denominations and groups. I have previously labeled it the "Blessing Movement"- It's 'streams' are severally identifiable as Howard Browne Ministries, the Toronto Blessing, Sunderland Outpouring and Pensacola Revival. This is, to me, one and the same movement in various forms.

GIDEON'S ARMY

The second army I saw however, portrays an altogether different picture. Here is an army fully prepared, awaiting instruction. It is not yet mobile. The battalion (in military terms about 10,000 men) was labeled Gideon's army. It represents the refined, the chosen, the remnant church. This second army is not yet marching. They are stable, focused, balanced and awaiting instruction. They have NOT been given their marching orders! Gideon and his men were exhorted: "Go in this might of yours and deliver Israel... I will be with you and you shall strike down the Midianites" (Judg 6:14,15).

Note there is an explicit command to strike down the enemies of Israel, or for the church, the devil and his powers - not the church!

CHAPTER SEVEN

A CHRISTIAN CIVIL WAR?

Way back In May 1996, Rick Joyner published an article entitled "Civil War in the Church" – and some of his most popular books also contain this theme. He issued a call to "fight until there was a complete victory. The definition of a complete victory in this war would be the complete overthrow of the Accuser of the Brethren's strongholds in the church." By this, it seemed, he meant an overthrow of the ones who wanted to "test the spirits" or to warn against deception. And a "great war" was to be fought against these people. When Lakeland came along a huge clamor for this Civil War was again raised by it's supporters. (Though now that everything has fallen apart, I'd love to know who they actually think "won").

In July 2008, just before the Lakeland revival totally collapsed, Lee Grady addressed this 'warlike' attitude in an article entitled, "Can We Avoid a Charismatic Civil War?" Below are some extracts:

I'll admit I was not paying too much attention to these Civil War predictions 10 years ago. But I was jolted into reality in May after I wrote an online column in which I raised honest questions about some of Bentley's teachings and techniques. Even though I celebrated his passion and zeal, and praised God for the healings that were reported in Lakeland, I was immediately branded a revival critic and banished to the Gray camp... now I realize that some people really want a war. They want the charismatic movement to split right down the middle. They imply that all those who do not embrace 100 percent of the current movement in Lakeland are "old wineskins" that cannot be used by God in the coming revival.

I want to plead with everyone in our movement to reconsider the whole Civil War scenario. Instead of rattling sabers and stockpiling gunpowder, maybe we need to take steps in the opposite direction:.. Let's accept one another... Let's admonish one another.... Let's pray for one another...

Below are my own comments that I sent out in reply to Grady's piece at the time:

I am just as strongly against a "Christian Civil War" as Lee Grady, but there are certain things in his approach that I just cannot agree with. Back in 1996, when Rick Joyner came out with his Civil War prophecy I even wrote an article on it entitled "WHY I OPPOSE the CIVIL WAR". (-A pretty outdated article now, but I am just as opposed today as I was then). I have never believed in such a thing - especially when it was essentially a call for the Prophetic/Toronto camp to try and "drive out" those who oppose them - right out of the church. It always seemed an utterly ill-advised and disastrous course to me - to put out a call like that just because people are opposing or questioning the "manifestations" that you are involved with. Is that any excuse for trying to "drive" them out? -I felt quite sad and shocked by it.

But Lee is right. There is a lot of "aggression" around right now - and it always happens when these kinds of movements come along. People get aggressive and nasty on both sides. I noticed it with Toronto and I am noticing it now. Suddenly everyone wants to "bash" each other. They want to make it "personal"...

Do I want to be attacking Lakeland or Todd Bentley in that way? No - I want no part of it at all. I believe we can raise the issues and bring forth the facts and "test the spirits" without resorting to any of these tactics. And our battle is not with flesh and blood anyway - it is with spiritual deception in "high places". So I am not at "war" with Todd Bentley. I will be as polite and reasonable as I can - while still putting forth the TRUTH about what I regard as dangerous heresy.

And here is where Lee Grady and I begin to differ... It sounds so loving and "tolerant" to speak of unity and say things like 'Can't we all just get along?" But this is not true biblical unity - which is based on TRUTH.

The fact is, Jesus said, "I have come not to bring peace but a sword." There is sometimes a division or separating that occurs over major issues which is unavoidable - and in fact can be totally necessary... It happened with Jesus all the time.

So I can well believe that there may come some kind of separation in the Charismatic movement. But let it not be because we ourselves are trying to "drive" people out or slinging mud - or engaging people in ways that are harsh or bitter. Let us preach the truth in love, and if there is to be a separation, let God Himself bring it about...

So do I believe that God Himself did begin to act soon afterward – to dethrone the false and expose all this spiritual pollution to the light? Yes – I do. I have believed for a long time that a massive "shaking" of leadership was coming to the Body of Christ – that God Himself would come to set order in His house – to "re-take" the ship, so to speak. Did the collapse of Lakeland (and the false "apostles" reputation) perhaps represent the start of this process? Maybe it did. As in the classic Old Testament parallel, I believe the era of 'Saulish' leadership must end, and that of the 'Davids' must begin. (Of which there are many – waiting in the wings).

A MASSIVE CHANGING OF THE GUARD

It may sound harsh, but there is nothing "personal" in this. I simply believe that what happened at Lakeland was the most shocking and unexpected "take-down" in modern church history. And it happened right before the TV cameras of all Christendom. I am not just talking about Todd Bentley here. I am talking about the top "apostles and prophets" of the entire Charismatic world. When they got up on stage to endorse that movement, and just weeks later we saw the entire thing begin to crumble and fall apart in the worst possible way – that was something I have never seen before in my lifetime. I don't believe we have ever seen God turn on His own top leadership en masse like that. Individuals have fallen – yes – but never this.

In many ways you would have to say it was a sad and terrifying sight. God is not playing games any more. His gloves are off.

So if the 'Saul-David' parallel holds, what follows next? Well, the Bible tells us:

"Now there was a long war between the house of Saul and the house of David: but David waxed stronger and stronger, and the house of Saul waxed weaker and weaker..." (2 Sam 3:1).

It is very possible that this is what we will now see playing out: The very process prophesied in Scripture- "The kingdom shall be taken from you and given to another, bringing forth the fruits thereof." God has had enough of deception holding sway over His church. Expect this "changing of the guard" to take place at every level of leadership - from local right up to international. Watch for it actually taking place.

Perhaps the time has come for the good shepherds - the "Davids" to arise – prepared for years in the wilderness for this time. (As I said, there are many of them). What is a 'good shepherd'? Someone who feeds the sheep 'good food' and who lays down his life to protect the sheep from the wolves. From now on, expect the house of David – the house of the "good shepherds" – to grow stronger and stronger, and the house of Saul to grow weaker and weaker. The Lord Himself will take the field - to fight on behalf of Truth. And woe betide those who stand in His path.

I am convinced that we are about to see Jesus violently re-take His church - and I believe in many cases He will use the 'word of the Lord' to do it – prophets and messengers speaking a piercing, "shaking" word. God will take back His own Body with great violence. This 'Shaking' has already begun.

As we have seen, there has been a lot of "presumption" in the church. The titles of 'prophet' and "apostle" have been bandied around too readily by too many. We are about to find out who gained their title and position by "presumption" and who is the real deal. These Last Days are prophesied as the most deceptive, seductive and dangerous period in all history. And God must have discerning leaders to guide His people through such treacherous seas.

RICK JOYNER REPLIES

Ironically, years ago Rick Joyner wrote a reply to my article, "Why I Oppose the Civil War," which we published at the time. It is pretty interesting to read his comments in light of recent events. His letter was dated August 28, 1996:

Dear Andrew,

I appreciate you sending me the article "Why I Oppose The 'Civil War'". I think that I do understand your position...

"There was a long war between the house of Saul and the house of David..." (II Sam.3:11)...

Most unfortunately, this war is already upon us. You have already shown that you will take sides, but are you really taking the side that you should be on? We are not warring against flesh and blood, and God forbid that we should see any brother as an enemy, even if they are trapped in deception, but just as I witnessed recently in Central Europe, this has been going on for a long time now, the present reformation of the church will rend many hearts, and organizations, just as the previous ones have, but truth will prevail. The end result, even between the houses of Saul and David, will be a true union of them.

Yours in Him, Rick Joyner.

I hope and pray that Mr Joyner is right about this eventual "union".

But sadly it appears that it was he who tragically ended up fighting on the "wrong side."

97

THE TRUTH ABOUT "JOEL'S ARMY"

As my friend Robert Holmes pointed out in his vision of "Joel's Army and Gideon's Army," the Scriptures openly declare Joel's army to be an army of LOCUSTS, which sweeps through immediately prior to the genuine Revival, devouring and destroying every good thing in the land. That is why I have always been puzzled why the 'River' movement wants to call itself "Joel's Army."

In Joel we see God Himself unleash this great army of locusts – devouring everything – then He drives the locusts away and later sends a great outpouring of His Spirit "upon all flesh". (If you don't believe me, just read the book of Joel for yourself. It is very clear. There can simply be no dispute about it). So why were we told that joining up with Joel's Army was such a desirable thing? And why did Paul Cain reportedly see visions of the words, "JOEL'S ARMY IN TRAINING" over the Kansas City Prophets' building when he first came across them?

Is it possible that this army of locusts has now done it's job of "devouring" for the last 20 years? Did God deliberately allow this, to "test" the church and her leaders? And is He now in the process of driving this "invasion" into the sea?

Years ago, before the 'Toronto blessing' arrived, a friend of mine from New Zealand was given a powerful dream. In it, he found himself in a large auditorium full of people. Many of them appeared spiritually 'fat' and overfed (including many of the leaders), while the rest seemed small in comparison. At the front of the auditorium he saw people falling down, laughing and crying, etc, and the words that were clearly spoken to him to describe what he was seeing were: "LAODICEAN REVIVAL". He noticed that it was essentially the large, overfed looking people who were really becoming 'caught up' in this laughing, crying and falling. In the dream, my friend was taken and seated with the small people. And as he watched, a great gulf began to appear between the large people (who were still caught up in their "Laodicean revival") and the little people, who were being steadily drawn away from this scene until a yawning gulf had developed between the two groups. Suddenly a great tide of young people flooded in all around these 'little' people, and they began to minister to them in the power of Jesus Christ. He knew that this was the beginning of the true Revival.

This dream is confirmed by the well-known allegory, "Escape from Christendom" (published by Morningstar many years ago) which also contains two revivals – one counterfeit and the other genuine. It also seems to fit in perfectly with the pattern found in the book of Joel.

SHOCKING FACTS ABOUT "TARES"

Of course, we all know Jesus' parable of the Tares and the Wheat. Tares are plants that look just like wheat until Harvest time - when it turns out that they were counterfeit. Awhile ago I learnt some facts about 'Tares' that truly shocked and surprised me.

When you look up the word "Tares" on Wikipedia, it comes back with the equivalent plant named "Darnel." This is exactly correct according to most Biblical authorities. The Tares are almost always considered to be the weed Darnel – also known as "false wheat" which grows plentifully in the whole region around Israel. Here is what Wikipedia says about it:

It bears a close resemblance to wheat until the ear appears ... It parasitizes wheat fields. The French word for darnel is "ivraie"... which expresses that weed's characteristic of making one feel poisoned with drunkenness, and can cause death. This characteristic is also alluded to in the scientific name (Latin temulentus = drunk)... The plant is mentioned in... the Parable of the Tares in the Gospel of Matthew.

So is this identification of Tares with "drunkenness" noted elsewhere? Yes – many Bible dictionaries and encyclopedias say exactly the same thing. In fact, the Faussett Bible Cyclopedia states that, *"when mixed with wheat flour [it] causes dizziness, intoxication, and paralysis"* and says that bearded darnel is known as *"the only deleterious grain"* among all the grasses.

On the giant website "Botanical.com" we read: " *It is recorded to have produced all the symptoms of drunkenness: a general trembling, followed by inability to walk, hindered speech and vomiting. For this reason the French call Darnel: 'Ivraie,' from Ivre (drunkenness)."*

Out of all the weed-type grasses, Tares are seemingly the only ones that produce this deadly "drunken" effect. Isn't that amazing? In the parable of the Wheat and the Tares in Matt 13, Jesus states that his "enemy" sows tares amongst the true wheat. Then He says:

"Let both grow together until the harvest: and in the time of harvest I will say to the reapers, Gather ye together first the tares, and bind them in bundles to burn them: but gather the wheat into my barn" (Mt 13:30).

I guess I don't need to point out the possible parallels with today's "Drunkenness"/ River movement. What an alarming insight – if it does have relevance to what we have seen today!

CHAPTER EIGHT
TRUE VS. FALSE REVIVAL

One of the things that really bugs me about the last 20 years is the total corruption of the word "Revival" and all that it stands for. As someone who has studied Revivals for many years, this seems like a complete travesty to me. So what, in essence, is real Revival – historically speaking? Well, the simplest way to explain it is "GOD COMING DOWN." Yes – God coming down in all His throneroom majesty and holiness.

The prophet Isaiah tells us exactly what His holy throneroom presence is like: "I saw also the Lord sitting upon a throne, high and lifted up... And one cried to another and said, Holy, holy, holy is the LORD of hosts: The whole earth is full of his glory. And the posts of the door moved at the voice of him that cried, and the house was filled with smoke" (Is 6:1-5, KJV).

It is this awesome sense of God's holy presence that saturates every real Revival and makes men fall on their faces and repent. Today we have a very frothy, shallow concept of what 'Revival' is – but the real thing has always been an invasion of this unspeakable holiness of almighty God. And it has always led to the cry, "God have mercy on me, a sinner." All the way down the centuries, true Revival has been a flood of purity, holiness and repentance aimed at cleaning out the church and restoring her to all that she is meant to be in the earth.

As the famous Revivalist and missionary Jonathan Goforth stated: *"We cannot emphasise too strongly our conviction that all hindrance in the church is due to sin."* And Frank Bartleman of the Azusa Street Revival wrote: *"The depth of revival will be determined exactly by the depth of the spirit of repentance."* Jonathan Edwards of the First Great Awakening in America was renowned for his famous sermon "Sinners in the Hands of an Angry God." It is recorded that as he preached it, *"the assembly appeared bowed with an awful conviction of their sin and danger. There was such a breathing of distress and weeping that the preacher was obliged to speak to the people and desire silence that he might be heard."* Many were seen holding themselves up against pillars and the sides of the pews, as though they felt themselves sliding into hell.

Another leader in that Awakening was Gilbert Tennant. It was said of his preaching that *"he seemed to have no regard to please the eyes of his hearers with agreeable gestures, not their ears with delivery, nor their fancy with language; but to aim directly at their hearts and consciences, to lay open their ruinous delusions, show them their numerous secret, hypocritical shifts in religion and drive them out of every deceitful refuge... His preaching was frequently both terrible and searching."* The results of this kind of preaching were often very powerful. As one pastor observed: *"Great numbers cried aloud in the anguish of their souls. Several stout men fell as though a cannon had been discharged and a ball made its way through their hearts."*

This has almost always been the character of true Revival preaching, from the Book of Acts right down to the present. On the day of Pentecost it was Peter accusing the Jews to their face of 'crucifying the Messiah' that caused them to be 'cut to the heart' and to cry out, "Men and brethren, what shall we do?" (Acts 2:36-37). And the Bible states that three thousand people were converted that day after hearing this one Spirit-fired sermon. Later in Acts we read of Paul's fearless preaching to governor Felix: "And as he reasoned of righteousness, temperance and judgment to come, FELIX TREMBLED..." (Acts 24:25).

That's right – true Revival preaching is the preaching of "Sin, righteousness and judgment"! (Jn 16:8). Nothing less will do. It is bold preaching, courageous preaching, life-risking preaching. And our generation has heard almost nothing like it. Such was the preaching of the Finneys, the Whitefields and the Wesleys of old. And such preaching must be heard again in our time.

True Revival is the mighty presence of a holy God sweeping in. As Amy Carmichael said of the 1905-6 Revival in India:

"Soon the whole upper half of the church was on its face on the floor, crying to God, each boy and girl, man and woman oblivious of all others. The sound was like the sound of waves or strong wind in the trees... The hurricane of prayer continued for over four hours."

"DEATH" BEFORE RESURRECTION

True Revival brings God's children to their knees. But after this deep cleansing, many Revivals have resulted in such over-whelming joy, praise and jubilation in those newly forgiven, that bystanders have often been astonished at the shouts of glory to God, the unrestrained worship and singing, etc. It is important to remember however, that such "righteousness, peace and joy in the Holy Spirit" is only truly possible amongst those who have come to this place by way of brokenness and deep repentance. There must always be 'death' before there can be resurrection.

If we see a movement today that does not involve the strong preaching of the 'Cross' – or conviction of sin – or the holiness of the Lord – then we know that that movement is not true Revival.

We need to seek God desperately for another Great Awakening – another real Revival in our day! We need the "John-the-Baptist" preachers back again. We need the Goforths and Wesleys of our time. Will you agonize and wrestle with God in prayer for such an outpouring, my friend? Will another wave of truth and cleansing sweep this generation before it is too late? Perhaps God is calling YOU to be just such a preacher. Pray and agonize before the Lord. Rend the heavens for God to come down. Only another heaven-sent Revival of this type will answer the church's desperate need in this hour.

COUNTERFEITS & FALSE MANIFESTATIONS

One thing that is very important to note is that there can be quite "unusual" things that occur when the real Holy Spirit of God descends upon people. Just like in the Book of Acts there can be tremendous cryings of distress over sin or 'trembling' under the fear of God, outbursts of joyous forgiveness, mass speaking in 'tongues', dreams, visions, etc.

The key is whether or not these things have a sense of God's holiness and truth about them – and whether these encounters are producing good fruit (i.e., godly results in people's lives) such as holy living and a greater hunger for God. We cannot just automatically write something off because it is "unusual". We have to 'test the spirits'.

For Revival leaders, the whole issue of counterfeits can be a very touchy area. These often happen on the fringes of a real Revival, but if they are not causing large-scale problems, then it can be best for the leaders not to draw too much attention to them. (Attempting to loudly correct relatively small-scale problems can sometimes make the people overly suspicious of ANYTHING unusual, thus making it hard for the Holy Spirit to work as well). However, if these counterfeits are flooding in on a large scale, it may be necessary for the leaders to bring open correction, using all the authority that God has given them.

I believe that the leadership in any true Revival will be very wary of encouraging soulishness in any way. I certainly can't imagine them using the kind of "tugging at the heart-strings" techniques so often seen today. All that is showy, all that is soulish, all that is shallow and that would wrap people up in a warm, positive, "feel-good" cocoon – all this God hates. And yet this kind of thing has become all too common in recent years. In my experience, very few Christians even seem to be able to tell this kind of Christianity from the real thing any more.

True Revival ministries will detest this kind of soulishness, hype and emotional manipulation. Their preaching (and their singing) will certainly not be in demonstration of personality, cleverness or showmanship, but rather, "in demonstration of the Spirit and of power" (1 Cor 2:4).

A MANIA FOR 'EXPERIENCES'

When the "manifestations" movement invaded the church in the mid-1990's, there were a lot of claims that it was somehow "just like Revivals of the past." I have to tell you, as someone who has been studying and writing on Revivals for years, this was an absolutely absurd claim. In fact, what this bizarre new movement most closely resembled was the COUNTERFEITS that often used to invade real Revivals – sometimes ruining and destroying them. As the well-known Revivalist John Wesley declared, *"At the first, revival is true and pure, but after a few weeks watch for counterfeits."*

It is a very significant fact that two of the greatest Revivals in history were virtually derailed and finished-off by "manifestation" movements that swept through at the time, while another had a very close call indeed. Both the First Great Awakening and the 1904 Welsh Revival were eventually crushed in this way, while the Second Great Awakening in Kentucky came very close to shipwreck. Yes, I will repeat what I just said: Two of these massive moves of God were basically finished-off by a flood of bizarre "manifestations" that swept through during the Revival. Many other moves of God have also had to contend with similar manifestations trying to get in. A lot of well-known Revivalists have commented on how difficult it was to keep the Revival on the rails and prevent the devil from bringing these kinds of things in.

As John Wesley said: *"Be not alarmed that Satan sows tares among the wheat of Christ. It has ever been so, especially on any remarkable outpouring of the Spirit; and ever will be, until the devil is chained for a thousand years. Till then he will always ape, and endeavor to counteract the work of the Spirit of Christ."*

False manifestations are often caused by believers seeking 'touches', blessings or experiences, rather than seeking God for His own sake. Some of these counterfeits are merely fleshly, while others can be downright demonic – especially if they involve a 'casting off of restraint' or a kind of "wildness." As the renowned revivalist Charles Finney stated, *"God's Spirit leads men by the intelligence, not through mere impressions... I have known some cases where persons have rendered themselves highly ridiculous, have greatly injured their own souls, and the cause of God, by giving themselves up to an enthusiastic and fanatical following of impressions."*

In both the First and Second Great Awakenings, as well as in some of the Pentecostal Revivals of more recent times, it has often been common for people to "fall down under the power of God". As you can imagine, this caused a great deal of controversy at the time. But I believe it was mostly of God. Please note that the Great Awakenings were mostly about conviction, repentance and holiness – not the seeking after of 'manifestations'. This is a true hallmark of Revival. As Pentecostal pioneer Frank Bartleman (of the Azusa Street Revival) wrote: *"A true 'Pentecost' will produce a mighty conviction for sin, a turning to God. False manifestations produce only excitement and wonder... Any work that exalts the Holy Ghost or the 'gifts' above Jesus will finally land up in fanaticism."*

In America, the most serious damage to the First Great Awakening occurred under pro-Revival preachers such as James Davenport and others who gained great notoriety for themselves with their excessive preaching and behavior – which definitely helped to bring an end to the whole Revival. As the Boston Evening Post wrote of Davenport: *"He has no knack at raising the Passions, but by a violent straining of his Lungs, and the most extravagant wreathings of his Body, which at the same time that it creates Laughter and Indignation in the most, occasions great meltings, screamings, crying, swooning and Fits in some others... they look'd more like a Company of Bacchanalians after a mad Frolick than sober Christians who had been worshipping God..."* These and other goings-on soon brought such controversy upon the whole Revival, that the Great Awakening ended in a deluge of bitter arguments and disputes. Surely one of the devil's all-time favorite methods for killing Revivals stone-dead. It had lasted just three or four years.

James Davenport actually made a public apology for these excesses in 1744, but by then it was far too late and the Revival was over.

Just over 50 years later, the Second Great Awakening centered in Kentucky came very close to suffering a similar fate. As usual, in the beginning this was a tremendous move of conviction and repentance. And so it largely remained at the start. People would fall down under great conviction of sin, piercing the air with their cries. Then, after a time they would experience such forgiveness that they were flooded with joy. All of this is perfectly normal in Revivals. But after about a year, as the Revival reached Cane Ridge and the camp-meetings became much larger, some truly bizarre manifestations began to flood in, and for awhile they came to almost dominate the Revival. This came very close to shipwrecking the entire movement in the Western states.

As noted Revival historian Keith J. Hardman writes: *"Cane Ridge also witnessed the beginning of excesses that had been generally condemned... ever since the wild antics and frenzies of James Davenport and others had brought discredit on the Great Awakening of New England in the 1740's. Excesses, or 'enthusiasms,' were viewed with great distaste by most prorevival evangelists..."*

Fortunately for the Kentucky Revival, these more bizarre manifestations began to die out before they could do irreparable damage. But it was a very close call. As Hardman continues: *"At later camp meetings shouting, crying, and falling down were the only physical reactions to rousing preaching. With the release of tidal waves of feeling in those early camp meetings, however, convulsive physical 'exercises' became somewhat common.*

Hysterical laughter, occasional trances, the 'barking' exercise and the 'jerks'..."

Here is how T.W. Caskey, an eyewitness, described these earlier manifestations which had almost ruined the Revival: *"The whole congregation by some inexplicable nervous action would sometimes be thrown into side-splitting convulsions of laughter and when it started, no power could check or control it until it ran its course. At other times the nervous excitement set the muscles to twitching and jerking at a fearful rate and finally settle down to regular, straight-forward dancing. Like the 'Holy Laugh' it was simply ungovernable until it ran its course. When a man started laughing, dancing, shouting or jerking, it was impossible for him to stop until exhausted nature broke down in a death-like swoon..."*

The same writer goes on to tell how a number of people slowly began to question whether such things really were the work of the Holy Spirit. They began to search the Scriptures and 'test the spirits' a lot more than they had been, and these more bizarre manifestations began to die out. This was very fortunate, as they had come close to bringing disrepute and disaster upon the whole movement. The Revival was able to sweep on without them after that. And it was to continue for another six years – maybe longer. Unlike the First Great Awakening, these kinds of excesses had not managed to kill the Revival stone dead.

However, it is a fact that these early Kentucky manifestations were notorious for decades afterwards, tainting the whole concept of 'revival' for many people. Even modern music historian Steve Turner writes of the Kentucky camp-meetings that the crowds would *"go into trances, writhe on the ground and even bark like dogs."* He doesn't mention that originally these gatherings had been for strong preaching and deep repentance. You see, it is often the bizarre and damaging elements that are remembered the longest. What a shame.

History shows that such counterfeits and excesses have often flooded in towards the end of a true Revival, when the devil has been trying to get in and completely destroy or discredit it. This happened to the 1904 Welsh Revival – and to the First and Second Great Awakenings as we have seen. The Welsh Revival only lasted about 18 months!

It should be obvious by now that there is absolutely NO WAY that Revivalists such as Finney, Wesley, Bartleman, Roberts, etc, would have condoned a "manifestations" movement such as the one we have seen in the last 20 years – with very little emphasis on repentance or holiness – but rather on bizarre and outlandish manifestations. In fact, what we have seen in recent times is whole movements made up of the very things that they were trying to KEEP OUT of their own Revivals! It is the "counterfeits" that have taken over. I find it ridiculous in the extreme when modern writers try to prove the validity of these manifestations by pointing to past Revivals and saying, "These things happened back then too." Yes – they did! They happened when counterfeits and excesses were trying to flood in and ruin real moves of God. All the great revivalists would tell you so.

Obviously, many similar deceptions have become all too prevalent in the Prophetic and Charismatic movements of today. In fact, as a student of Revival history I would have to say that both of these movements now display many of the hallmarks of "fallen" moves of God. Don't we realize that much of the deception prophesied for the last days must clearly arise from WITHIN THE CHURCH?

In the times we live in, it is essential for Christians to hone their discernment as much as possible. I myself certainly believe in the moving of the Holy Spirit and the gifts of the Spirit and true signs and wonders from God. And I cannot doubt that such things will have a definite part to play in any true Revival – just as they did in the Book of Acts – which is full of healings and miracles of every kind. But the Bible does clearly state that the Last Days are an age of deception. And in times like these a real Revival can only survive if it is deeply grounded in the truth, the holiness and the discernment of God.

TRUE & FALSE APOSTLES

One last thing that we must discuss before leaving this "True vs. False" chapter is the modern movement known as the "New Apostolic Reformation" – and other similar movements around the world. To be fair, I am not against the concept of 'Apostles,' just as I am not against the concept of Prophets – so long as they are the real thing. But I have a real problem with what amounts to Charismatic "Good Old Boys" networks carving up the Body of Christ into 'territories' to reign over – and printing business cards with the word 'Apostle' so they can form hierarchies over the church.

Are these men truly and fully "New Testament" apostles? I don't think so. And I believe the very fact that God publicly embarrassed and humiliated their movement at Lakeland should speak volumes. No-one can deny that it was these 'New Apostles' who convened the public 'Commissioning' of Bentley that went so horribly wrong. To me, that was God making a statement about what He thinks of their "apostolic" movement! But these guys never learn. They are still at it – forming ever-wider "networks" to set hierarchies over the church. And I believe it is something that God hates. Do not be surprised to see Him act with shocking suddenness again to send it all reeling. These guys still haven't got the message. To call oneself an "apostle" over the church is the height of arrogance unless it is God Himself who has done the calling.

In Revelation 2, the church of Ephesus was strongly commended by Jesus: "You have tested those who say they are apostles and are not, and have found them liars…" (Rev 2:2). Isn't it high time that the modern church did the same?

CHAPTER NINE

BILL JOHNSON & THE NEW AGE

As we have seen, after the debacle surrounding Lakeland and Todd Bentley, things seemed to quiet down a little on the 'invasion' front. All except for one huge mega-ministry that just kept going from strength to strength. Of course I am speaking here of Bethel church in Redding, California – led by Bill Johnson.

Even though he had stood on that stage in Lakeland, and publicly endorsed and defended Todd Bentley (even after his marriage breakup), seemingly Bill Johnson was totally immune from the fallout that ensued. (Rick Joyner was not so fortunate).

On a worldwide scale, Johnson has become something of a Charismatic megastar. In the Southern Hemisphere in particular, his influence is overwhelming. Every year he holds conferences in nations like New Zealand, Australia and Singapore – where thousands of pastors and leaders hang on every word he utters. Without doubt he is one of the most influential figures in the Charismatic world today. And with the 'Jesus Culture' music outreach, he has vast numbers of Christian youth under his influence also. Bethel is an absolute juggernaut in every sense. And for many, Bill Johnson can do no wrong.

In a previous chapter we published the testimony of a young woman who had graduated from the Bethel School of Supernatural Ministry. The things she told us about Bethel are confirmed from many sources. The constant 'drunken' behavior, hysterical laughter, shaking, jerking, orbs, "fire tunnels," etc. And the never-ending talk of bizarre angel encounters and trips to the 'third heaven.' By now I'm sure every reader is all-too familiar with such goings-on.

But at Bethel it goes a lot deeper. For not only do they allow subtle New Age practices in the back door. Bethel now actually endorses full-blown New Age activities openly – claiming that they are simply "stealing back" what the devil stole in the first place!

A MOST ASTOUNDING BOOK

In 2012 an astonishing book was published that should have rung alarm bells right around the globe. It was called, *'The Physics of Heaven'* – co-authored by Bill Johnson's administrative assistant Judy Franklin with a foreword by Bethel pastor Kris Vallotton. Bill Johnson and his wife, Beni, contributed three chapters to the book and it was publicly endorsed by Banning Liebscher of Jesus Culture. In every way it was as close as you could get to an "official" Bethel publication. (It is still sold on the Bethel website to this day).

The contents of this work are absolutely astounding. The book's blurb says it all: *"Exploring the mysteries of God in sound, light, vibrations, frequencies, energy, and quantum physics."* But this is far from a work of 'science'. It is mystical New Age weirdness – designed to introduce bizarre pagan ideas into the mainstream of Christianity.

There are eleven contributors to the book, including Bob Jones, Larry Randolph, Cal Pierce (of 'Healing Rooms' fame), Jonathan Welton, and of course, Bill and Beni Johnson. The other co-author of the work, Ellyn Davis stated that, *"[The contributors of the book] all agree that the next move of God will cause a shift at the deepest level of who we are—perhaps the very 'vibrational level' that the New Age movement has been exploring. They also all agree that there are precious truths hidden in the New Age that belong to us as Christians..."* Ms. Davis also wrote in the book: *"I could not find a single Christian leader who shared a similar interest in finding out if there were truths hidden in the New Age. Now we are beginning to hear more and more revelation that is in line with what New Agers have been saying all along and we are hearing more and more teaching about Christians "taking back truths" from the New Age."* Truths from the New Age? Are you serious? If people's alarm bells aren't going off yet – they should be. Have you ever heard anything so blatant?

Please remember that this is as close as you can get to an "officially sanctioned" publication coming out of Bethel. As Bethel pastor Kris Vollotton said in his foreword to the work: *"In this powerful book, Judy Franklin and Ellyn Davis assemble a team of seers who peer behind the curtain of creation to reveal the mysterious nature of our Creator... Through their collective intelligence these seers have emerged with new perspectives never before pondered."*

So what are these new perspectives "never before pondered?" Well, as we have seen, the main one is that even the most pagan of New Age practices can now be "taken back" and used by Christians. Even though occult practices of this type are specifically forbidden in Scripture (eg. Deut 18:10-12), we are now led to understand that all is well – and these things that Christians down the ages have always viewed as evil are "perfectly fine" to bring into the church.

I don't know about you, but I consider this to be one of the most dangerous things I have ever heard. So what exact kinds of practices are these authors advocating?

Well, in the chapter entitled, 'Authentic vs Counterfeit,' we are told by contributor Jonathan Welton, *"I have found throughout Scripture at least 75 examples of things that the New Age has counterfeited, such as having a spirit guide, trances, meditation, auras, power objects, clairvoyance, clairaudience, and more. These actually belong to the church, but they have been stolen and cleverly repackaged."*

So are you telling me that Christians should be looking for 'auras' around peoples' heads, trying to enter "trance" states, listening to spirit guides, gaining power from "talisman"-type objects just as pagans do, seeking "out-of-body" experiences, etc? From the book it is clear that these are EXACTLY the kinds of things that the authors are advocating.

Little wonder that all of this lines up perfectly with the absolute explosion of New Age practices that the devil has been infiltrating into the church generally. What the New Agers call "transcendental meditation" has been cleverly repackaged as 'contemplative prayer.' What they call "astral travel" has been repackaged as 'spirit travel' in the church. All of the "portals" and visualizations and 'angelic' guides are simply direct imports from the New Age religion. And a lot of this is being taught to CHRISTIAN TEENAGERS in places like Bethel.

I do not believe we have ever lived in an age that is as dangerous as the one we are in right now. As we have seen, Jesus warned that the deception in the last days would be so great that even the "very elect" might be deceived. "Lying signs and wonders" and 'seducing spirits' become commonplace. "Angels of light" become ever-more active. Where is the discernment?

"GOOD VIBRATIONS"

Of course, all of this sheds new light on some of the "interesting" statements that Bill Johnson has made over the years. In a 2006 book Johnson wrote: *"Many prominent pastors and conference speakers add fuel to the fire of fear by assuming that because the New Age promotes it, its origins must be from the devil."* If the 'New Age' promotes it? What are you saying here, Bill?

As Johnson's administrative assistant Judy Franklin wrote: *"Bill Johnson writes that we can't just camp around old truth, but should seek new truths for our generation and then preserve those truths for the generations that follow."* Just what exact kinds of "new truths" are we talking about here? Judy Franklin also wrote: *"It wasn't that I wanted to become a New Ager, I just wanted to find out if maybe they had uncovered some truths the church*

114

hadn't." What a shocking statement! She went to the New Age to uncover truths that she felt the church lacked. What on earth?

The list of chapter headings in the book, *'The Physics of Heaven'* is also quite instructive: *Chapter 6 – "Good Vibrations," Chapter 8 – "The God Vibration," Chapter 12 – "Quantum Mysticism."* And some of the sub-headings are even more astounding: *"Dolphins and Healing Energy," "The Power of Color," "Human Body Frequencies,"* etc. What kind of 'Christian' book is this? And what does it say about the real Bethel behind the scenes?

Perhaps this could explain some of Bob Jones' strange comments to Todd Bentley at the Lakeland revival: *"As I watch you, you VIBRATE. You know there are two portals, clockwise and counter-clockwise. When you vibrate you close demonic vibration. Counter-clockwise vibration is demonic. The vibration is healing."* Is there anything remotely biblical about any of this "good vibrations" stuff? No! Most of it comes directly out of the Hippie/ New Age handbook. So what is it doing in the church?

This might also explain the very strange case of the tuning fork and Mrs Beni Johnson (wife of Bill Johnson). Beni Johnson has a whole history of strange beliefs and practices – yet she is CO-PASTOR of Bethel alongside her husband Bill.

In her 'Life and Wellness' blog on July 6, 2012, Beni wrote: *"I was talking with Ray Hughes the other day and was telling him about using a 528 HZ tuning fork as a prophetic act. Someone told me that this tuning fork is called the tuning fork of LOVE... One thing about this 528 HZ tuning fork is that science tells us that the sound of this fork brings healing."* (Please note that crystals and tuning forks are used in NEW AGE therapy – and have nothing to do with Christianity in any way. After all, why do we need tuning forks when we have the name of JESUS?)

"WAKEY WAKEY"

Beni Johnson had also written another controversial blog post in March 2009 on the topic of 'WAKING UP ANGELS.' The saddest part of it all is that they are completely serious about this stuff. Take a look-

"In the last couple of months, I personally have become more aware of the angelic activity in this realm. One of those times was when we were on a prayer trip to Arizona... One morning as we were driving up over Tehachapi Pass and coming down into the Mojave Desert, I began to feel angels. The closer we got, the stronger the impression felt. I could see them everywhere!.. I announced this to the group and said, "We have got to stop! We have to stop somewhere..." As we drove around a corner I said, "I think that we are going to wake up some angels here...""

"We knew we were to turn around, get out of the RV and wake up the angels. I wish I could convey to you the energy and the quickness of how God was working. We jumped out of the RV, I blew the shofar and rang the bell, and we yelled "WAKEY WAKEY." We got back into the RV and drove off. As we drove off, hilarious laughter broke out! We were stunned at the speed at which this all took place and were spinning from the adventure and the angelic activity. What in the world had just happened?! Heaven collided with earth. Woo hoo!!

"Since that time, there has been a stirring in me to awaken the angels for use in this Kingdom reign that is upon us here on earth. I have shared these two stories in other places and have done a prophetic act of waking up the angels: having everybody cry out, "WAKEY WAKEY!" I know it is strange but it is very effective... One of our gals who enjoys God's angels... gets pretty wacked when they are around..."

The reference that Beni makes here to "Heaven colliding with earth" is, of course, directly tied to Bill Johnson's most famous teaching on "When Heaven Invades Earth." Clearly, this is the kind of thing they mean when they use that phrase. So if we get with their program so-to-speak, we too can go around "waking up angels" and getting "pretty wacked" when these angels are around. All of this may sound silly or ridiculous to some, but behind it all is a very dark cloud of occultic and New Age heresy that these people are introducing into the Body of Christ. And their influence is enormous. (And worldwide).

If you really want to understand where Bethel is coming from and what is behind the things they teach, I strongly recommend that you obtain a copy of *'The Physics of Heaven.'* It is about as mystical and New Age as a so-called "Christian" book can get.

JESUS CULTURE & GLOBAL YOUTH

Jesus Culture is a music outreach, originally formed and based (for many years) out of Bethel – and it is targeted mainly at young people worldwide. It has been enormously successful. In fact, if you look on Facebook you will see that Jesus Culture has more than two million followers on that website alone. This is quite rare even for secular music stars. An incredible level of popularity. And of course, even though Jesus Culture moved to Sacramento in 2013, they are utterly steeped in the Bethel culture from which they sprang. (Maybe a little more on the 'subtle' side). As noted earlier, the leader of Jesus Culture, Banning Liebscher, publicly endorsed the book, *'The Physics of Heaven'* when it came out.

The main worship leaders at Bethel are Brian and Jenn Johnson, who have also released many music albums. Jenn Johnson is famous for her somewhat outrageous statements about the Holy Spirit. She has often declared from the stage that she views the Holy Spirit as being like "the genie from Aladdin." She also describes the Holy Spirit as "blue-colored," courageous, "silly," funny, 'sneaky' and "fun." To hear her talk so glibly about the Holy Spirit of God in this way is quite disturbing – especially likening Him to a 'genie'. Whether she has heard of the concept of "blaspheming the Holy Spirit" is not known.

OCCULTIC HERESY

The things we have been looking at in this chapter are very serious indeed. What could be deadlier than introducing New Age practices or beliefs into Christ's precious church? Remember, when

Nadab and Abihu offered "profane fire" before the Lord in the Old Testament, they were consumed by God and died (Lev 10:1-2). This stuff is not a joke. So what of today's "profane" fire?

Bill Johnson is a very likeable, warm, charming man with many good things to say. Sadly I have come to believe he is also a very deceived individual – who is deceiving others on a mass scale. Is it really that hard to believe that in the last days a place like Bethel could become a center for New Age influence infiltrating the church? Isn't it just the kind of place the enemy would choose?

When we hear from first-hand sources over and over that young people in Bethel are passing through 'fire tunnels', chasing "orbs" of light (in Wicca these are called 'sprites'), opening heavenly "portals" to invite strange spirits in, jerking and laughing for hours, communing with bizarre 'angels,' practicing "spirit travel," etc. - doesn't it sound like some mystical New Age cult? None of this is Christian behavior at all. It has always been the Eastern mystery religions that have pursued this stuff – not Christianity. We have the name of JESUS. We don't need this demonic garbage! Why on earth would anyone think it is OK to repackage the 'dark arts' and bring them into Christianity?

And right around the world today there are countless leaders and ministries who carry this self-same 'polluted' anointing. People often write to me, asking about this 'name' or that name associated with this movement. But it is simply impossible to keep up with them all. There are thousands – all of them spreading pollution to varying degrees. This so-called "anointing" is everywhere.

So what can be done, I hear you ask? Well, one thing is certain. The Charismatic movement today is in such a state that only God can clean it out (if this is even possible any more). Many believe that the pollution now runs so deep that this movement is beyond saving. Maybe – but there are still many individuals within it whose eyes can be opened. And it is up to us to reach them. "Come out from among them," must be the cry. Jesus is returning for a spotless and unadulterated bride.

CHAPTER TEN

WANTED – THE REAL THING

In closing, I want to bring some "balance" to this book. After reading what we have said regarding the dangers of the "false," a lot of people may be wondering what is truly "OK" –what is really from the Holy Spirit?

For instance, does the Holy Spirit sometimes cause people to "fall down" under the power of God? Yes, as we discussed earlier – I believe sometimes He does. But He does not need to make some big "show" about it. And neither does He need men to "push" people over, either. There are counterfeits for everything.

What about the gifts of the Holy Spirit – like tongues, prophecy, healings, discernment and the casting out of demons, etc? Yes - I believe very strongly in ALL the gifts of the Holy Spirit. They are right the way through the New Testament. But the key is this word "Holy." The real gifts of God have a holiness and purity about them. You can sense this. As stated earlier, counterfeits tend to have a "weirdness" or ugliness about them.

Let me give you an example. I received the following account from a preacher in England several years ago: *"There were about 20 fellow ministers all gathered together in one large room at a local minister's house. We were introduced to the special guest... The next 3 hours were the weirdest three hours I have ever had to endure. We started listening to [her] testimony which seemed very powerful, next she spoke of the times that she meets with the Angel Gabriel and other spiritual beings, next we moved on to portals between this world and the next and then finally to how she was going to open up a portal to Heaven in the room that we were all in. Now things started to happen, really crazy things and strange noises... As [she] moved around the room ministering to individual people they were crashing to the ground, bouncing up and down, running around as if on fire and making all sorts of sounds. When she came to me she had no prophetic words for me and nothing happened to me so she just moved on. My Vineyard friend was the first to crash to the floor. Since that day his church has taken on a different guise, it is not the same church any more."*

Please notice that the PREACHING was different from true Biblical preaching – and the SPIRIT that the lady was ministering in did not seem like the pure Holy Spirit. Can you tell the difference?

We need to watch out for preachers who bring unbiblical or "New Age"-sounding terms into their preaching – or who talk about "angels" all the time. Can people have true encounters with real angels? Yes - but always these beings that come from the presence of a Holy God carry His "holiness" with them. Angels in the Bible always carried this weighty presence of a Holy God. There is too much weirdness, ugliness and silliness in a lot of Christian meetings today. And I believe a lot of these encounters are not real angels at all.

Another thing to watch for is what is called "Contemplative" or 'centering' prayer. (Of course I am a big believer in prayer – but not this kind!) As Heidi Swander wrote: *"In its pure form, contemplative prayer is practiced by sitting still, quieting, and concentrating on your breathing and repeating a word of choice (maybe the name Jesus, for instance) over and over again. You're to concentrate on that word and your breathing, and work to eliminate all thoughts from your mind. Over a period of maybe 20 minutes -- and with practice -- you can enter into "the silence." Your mind is blank. You have, in fact, hypnotized yourself. And it is in "the silence" where "God" allegedly speaks to you. According to the testimony of one former, now-redeemed New Ager I recently read, this is the exact method used by New Agers and Eastern mystics to enter an altered state of consciousness that opens a person up to demonic influence."*

As we have seen, there is a lot of this New-Agey kind of stuff entering the church right now under the guise of "ancient prayer techniques" and 'visualization,' etc. Let the people of God beware!

SO WHO CAN BE TRUSTED?

A lot of Christians today have become so concerned about the False that they will no longer go forward in meetings or allow hands to be laid on them for prayer, etc. I truly believe this is taking things too far. So is it usually safe to go forward for healing and so-on? Absolutely! If the preaching is sound and biblical and the preacher is not putting on some big "show." As long as he has not gotten some weird "impartation" from one of these strange 'revival' meetings then he is probably fine. In fact, I am all for the real power of God being demonstrated in the earth! I wish we were seeing a lot MORE true healings and deliverances and miracles – not less! Jesus said, "These things will you do, and greater things than these"! (Jn 14:12).

Just think about the Book of Acts for a moment. Not only are there healings and miracles and demons being cast out right through the whole book, but there are also occasionally angels appearing with instructions from the Lord, and an abundance of dreams, visions and prophecies, etc. So we see that God is definitely a SUPER-NATURAL GOD. He does do "unusual" things. Angelic visitations DO HAPPEN. Prophetic signs DO OCCUR. But please notice that all of these things have a certain holy "character" about them. And that is the key right there. They have a holy character, because they come from a holy God.

I believe in a true Revival that has the piercing "word" of a John the Baptist or a Jonathan Edwards or a Charles Finney – accompanied by the most powerful MIRACLES that anyone has ever seen. I believe in a Revival like that - the "word and the Spirit joined." True, piercing 'holiness' preaching with real signs and miracles following. There is nothing wrong with that. In fact, it is

121

what the Book of Acts shows us again and again. Bring it back, Lord!

So please be discerning – but don't be afraid of the real supernatural power of God. Without it, we simply cannot reach this lost and dying world in the way that God has called us to. The devil wants us to be so afraid of the "counterfeit" that we run right over to the other extreme – where we don't want God's power or anything "unusual" at all. That is just as big a trap as the "Charismania" excesses on the other side. The devil loves to push us to extremes – either hyper-Charismania or dead orthodoxy. I believe in a powerful balance right in the middle – the "word and the Spirit" joined. That is where real Revival is to be found. Don't let the devil rob you by pushing you to either extreme, my friends!

Years ago as a young 17-year-old Baptist, God filled me with the Holy Spirit in a way that utterly revolutionized my life. Did I speak in "tongues"? Yes, I did! Was I filled with the love and holiness of God? Yes, I was! Do I expect others to speak in "tongues" when they receive this experience also? Yes – usually I do – just like in the Book of Acts! In one day I was utterly changed – filled with a hunger and desire for Jesus and His righteousness. It was truly a baptism of "holiness." So how did this occur? Through the "laying on of hands" – just like in the Bible! So please do not reject the laying on of hands or the gifts of the Holy Spirit, my friends. They are biblical, they are powerful and I believe we need to see MORE of them in today's world – not less!

REAL PROPHETS NEEDED

As I wrote soon after leaving the Prophetic movement in 2004:

Just because I have cut myself off from today's Prophetic movement does not mean that I believe there is no place for prophets in the church. In fact, I believe we need true prophets now more than ever. But you will notice that there has been a subtle shift in the use of the term "prophet" over the last 25 years, and I believe we need to get back to the original meaning. It was not long ago that when you spoke of a 'prophet' you were usually referring to someone like Keith Green, Leonard Ravenhill or David Wilkerson – someone who was crying out to the lukewarm church, "REPENT." And if you look down the annals of history, you will find that there has never been a true Prophetic movement that did not have this as its core message. Every true Prophetic movement, right from the Old Testament down through every Revival and Awakening that I have ever studied, has been a movement of REPENTANCE. And yet we find today a movement that calls itself "Prophetic" – but with spiritual 'revelations' and words of knowledge at its core. -No piercing word. This is the precise reason why it has gone off the rails. -It has abandoned its age-old message. It's 'word' has been corrupted.

I am convinced that God IS going to raise up true prophets in this hour to cry to the lukewarm church "Repent". There is a movement coming that is utterly different from that which we have seen. God is coming to clean house. The "shaking" has already begun. And the "John-the-Baptists" whom God has prepared in the caves and wildernesses are about to arise and speak His word – just as in every Great Awakening down through history.

Some people asked me if I was going to shut down our web-sites and email Lists. Not at all. The whole point of what we're doing is to call forth and encourage these "John-the-Baptists" whom God is raising up in this hour. We will not stop crying aloud until we see a great 'Repentance' Revival sweeping this nation from coast to coast.

And all I can say is "Amen" to what I said back then!

IN CONCLUSION

I believe we have now entered a time of great 'shaking' in the church – particularly at a leadership level. God is beginning a "clean out" and it will not be pretty. I also believe that there are two major spirits (at least) that need to be confronted and driven from the church. One is the spirit of 'Kundalini' (ironically more of a problem in the West) and the other is the spirit of 'Mammon' (ie. the "love of money") which has become utterly rampant across the continents of Africa, South America and parts of Asia. We are faced with a worldwide crisis in the church.

But as we have seen, God is not mocked. He has already begun to "clean house." And all we need to do is co-operate with Him. (And to do so in the right spirit). But there is no doubt that this is an hour for 'confrontation.' If ever there was a modern moment for "Elijah vs. the prophets of Baal," this is it. The 'false' has never been so dominant. The money preachers have never been so brazen. It is time for God to "shake". And He is, as we have seen. So are we ready to co-operate with Him? Are we willing to stick our neck on the line for Truth, even at the cost of our own reputation – and even our very lives? That is what it is going to take. God is looking for these bold servants right now – His "John the Baptists" – prepared for years in the wilderness for this time. Tell me, friend, might you be one of these?

For years our preachers have sown the seeds for this deception with their "cotton candy" gospel. No preaching of sin or judgment, no deep repentance or holiness. Just a diet of "sugar water". But all that has to change. For we are in the end times – the days of great seduction and deception, of "lying signs and wonders" – and there has never been a greater need for Truth than there is right now. Will you risk all to deliver it, my friend? Will you risk all to stand? "The Lord has need of thee." Will you respond?

VISIT OUR WEBSITE-

www.revivalschool.com

QUOTES AND REFERENCES

CHAPTER ONE

1. John Crowder's Mystic School - www.thenewmystics.com
2. J. Lee Grady, "Sloshed in the Spirit – It's Time to Get Sober", Oct 27, 2009 – www.charismamag.com/fireinmybones
3. David Lowe, 'The Ravers Who Get High on God', The Sun, 21 Jan 2010 - www.thesun.co.uk
4. Derek Prince, 'Protection from Deception', pg 15 – www.derekprince.com
5. Andrew Strom, 'Revival – We Need It' - Challenge Weekly, 26 Aug 1994.
6. Benny Hinn transcript - "PTL" telecast, Trinity Broadcasting Network, July 4, 1997. Distributed by CPI-EDG listserv – www.pentecostal-issues.org

CHAPTER TWO

1. New Age/ Gurus - ref: C. and S. Grof, "The Stormy Search for the Self". (See also, Christian "SCP Newsletter" volume 19:2, pg 14).
2. Robert Walker quote -www.pastornet.net.au/response/articles/107.htm
3. Shri Yogãnandji Mahãrãja source: 'Devatma Shakti (Kundalini): Divine Power' by Swami Vishnu Tirtha - www.cit-sakti.com/kundalini/kundalini-manifestations.htm
4. San Francisco Chronicle, 1991.
5. Franz Mesmer - ref: T. Bambridge, "Hypnotism Investigated", pg 93.
6. Peter Bell & Sherie testimonies – www.revivalschool.com
7. Geri McGhee - www.abidinglifeministries.org
8. 'Revival-Fire', DebyLynne & Brenda testimonies – revivalschool.com

CHAPTER THREE

1. John Kilpatrick – Source: S. Simpson, 'A Different Gospel?' - www.deceptioninthechurch.com/differ.html

2. 'An Interview with Evangelist Steve Hill' by Steve Beard, Good News Magazine.
3. Cathy Wood – Source: Jim Wies' distribution List, 26 April 1997.
4. 'New Wine Drinking Song' by Kathryn Riss - The 'New Wine' email List.
5. Paul Gowdy, 'The Toronto Deception'.

CHAPTER FOUR

1. 'The Four Standards,' Mike Bickle – Audio tape, KC Metro, 1991.
2. Royal D. Cronquist, 'Toronto' article, Mar 19, 1997.
3. Bob Jones at Lakeland - Transcript, May 13, 2008 - http://ischristsoontoreturn.wordpress.com/2009/05/13/transcript-of-todd-bentley-and-lakeland-stage-quotes/
3. Lynn, Pastor M.S, Jack, Johanna & Lucy – www.revivalschool.com
4. Dana Candler, "Deep Unto Deep - The Journey of the Embrace", pg 52, 84.
5. Sarah, M— and other testimonies – www.revivalschool.com
6. Mike Bickle dream, Feb 13, 2009 – Source: http://joannareyburn.com/mike-bickles-dream-february-13-2009 Original Source: www.ihop.org/Publisher/File.aspx?id=1000011101
7. Andrew Strom, 'I'm Leaving the Prophetic Movement,' 4 Nov 2004.

CHAPTER FIVE

1. Charisma Magazine - 'A Holy Ghost Outbreak in Florida', 23 April 2008 - www.charismamag.com
2. Lynn's testimony - www.revivalschool.com
3. Todd Bentley, 'Angelic Hosts' - www.etpv.org/2003/angho.html 4. Todd Bentley on CBN News – www.cbnnews.com
5. UK Report – 'Dudley Outpouring' ~ http://www.supernaturalliving.com/welcome.html
6. The Elijah List – www.elijahlist.com
7. J. Lee Grady, "Honest Questions About the Lakeland Revival", May 14, 2008 – www.charismamag.com/fireinmybones
8. J. Lee Grady, "An Appeal for Unity in a Divisive Season", May 28, 2008 – www.charismamag.com/fireinmybones
9. Charisma Magazine, "Leaders Commission Todd Bentley at 'Lakeland Outpouring'", Jun 23, 2008 - www.charismamag.com

10. C. Peter Wagner, 'Personal Report of Lakeland Outpouring,' June 25, 2008.
11. Robert Ricciardelli blog comments – www.jasonclark.ws & www.stevehickey.wordpress.com – July 14-16, 2008.
12. Robert Ricciardelli – Public Forum at www.RevivalSchool.com
13. J. Lee Grady, "Life After Lakeland: Sorting Out the Confusion," Aug 13, 2008 - www.charismamag.com/fireinmybones
14. Andrew Strom, 'Part 2 - Why I Left the Prophetic Movement.'
15. J. Lee Grady, "The Tragic Scandal of Greasy Grace," Mar 11, 2009 - www.charismamag.com/fireinmybones

CHAPTER SIX

1. Stanley Frodsham vision, 1965 –
http://brothermel.com/stanleyfrodshamrecordings.aspx
2. Richard Smith vision - Source: Integrity Teaching Services, 10 Hyde Park Close, Headingly, Leeds LS6 1SF, UK.
3. Robert Holmes vision, 1996 - http://stormharvest.com.au

CHAPTER SEVEN

1. Rick Joyner, 'Civil War in the Church,' May 1996 -
www.morningstarministries.org/Publisher/File.aspx?id=1000002723
2. J. Lee Grady, "Can We Avoid a Charismatic Civil War?" July 9, 2008 - www.charismamag.com/fireinmybones
3. Andrew Strom, "The Coming Great Reformation," pg 95-96.
4. 'Rick Joyner's Reply to the 'Civil War' Article', Aug 28, 1996.
5. Wikipedia – 'Tares' -
http://en.wikipedia.org/wiki/Lolium_temulentum
6. 'Tares', Bible Cyclopedia, A. R. Faussett, 1902, Trinity College, Dublin.
7. 'Darnel', Botanical.com -
www.botanical.com/botanical/mgmh/g/grasse34.html

CHAPTER EIGHT

1. Jonathan Goforth, 'By My Spirit'.
2. F. Bartleman, "Azusa Street", pg 19.
3. Jonathan Edwards – Source: 'True Revival and the Men God Uses' by H. Bonar, chapter one.

4. Gilbert Tennant – Source: 'A History of New England' by Isaac Backus.
5. Source: The Congregationalists By J. William T. Youngs, pg 83. 6. Amy Carmichael – Source: 'The Fire of Revival' by Derrick Harrison, pg 76.
7. John Wesley. Source: G. Strachan, "Revival - It's Blessings and Battles", pg 44.
8. John Wesley. Source: F. Bartleman, "Azusa Street", pg 45.
9. C.G. Finney, "Reflections on Revival", pg 66.
10. F. Bartleman, "Azusa Street", pg 86.
11. Boston Evening Post, ~1743.
12. Keith J. Hardman, "The Spiritual Awakeners", pg 138.
13. T.W. Caskey. Source: "Seventy years in Dixie" by F.D. Srygley.
14. Steve Turner, "Hungry for Heaven", 1988.

CHAPTER NINE

1. Ellyn Davis, 'The Physics of Heaven' (Double Portion Publishing, 2012).
2. Kris Vollotton, Foreword, 'The Physics of Heaven' (Double Portion Publishing, 2012).
3. Bill Johnson, 'Dreaming With God' (Destiny Image, 2006), pg 86.
4. Jonathan Welton, Chapter 5, 'The Physics of Heaven' (Double Portion Publishing, 2012).
5. Judy Franklin, 'The Physics of Heaven' (Double Portion Publishing, 2012).
6. Beni Johnson Blog - www.benijohnson.blogspot.com/

CHAPTER TEN

1. Heidi Swander, 'Beware of This Doctrine of Demons' - www.olivetreeviews.org
2. Andrew Strom, 'Part 2 – Why I Left the Prophetic Movement,' 2004.